A Life of One Thousand Blessings

Devotional Thought Journal

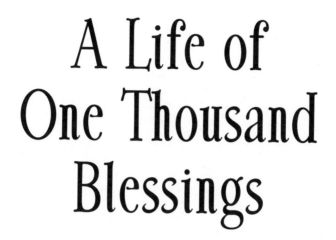

A Life of One Thousand Blessings

Devotional Thought Journal

BARBOUR BOOKS
An Imprint of Barbour Publishing, Inc.

Published by Barbour Books, an imprint of Barbour Publishing, Inc., 1810 Barbour Drive, Uhrichsville, Ohio 44683, www.barbourbooks.com

Our mission is to inspire the world with the life-changing message of the Bible.

 Member of the
Evangelical Christian
Publishers Association

Printed in China.

$\mathcal{I}$magine God had a quiet schedule one day. He looks down and sees you. Then He decides to give you 1,000 blessings.

Not wishes. I'm sure you can imagine the chaos and confusion that would result if the Almighty granted a flawed human being 1,000 wishes! No. Blessings. Beautiful, freely given, gifts.

The very idea is enough to inspire a "Wow!" Wouldn't life be wonderful if only the dear Lord could find time in His agenda to do that?

Well, it is! And He has! The Bible tells us so with around 400 verses addressing the subject of blessings. We just take them for granted at times.

This, easy to dip into at any point, journal contains a list of 1,000 real-life, everyday blessings—a fraction of those bestowed on us from heaven above—in the hope that they will help you look at creation, and the gifts God has filled it with, from a new, more appreciative perspective.

Each page has a dedicated space for you to add your thoughts or to record your very own blessings, and each is completed by a verse from scripture. . .something to ponder in your heart.

What does 1,000 blessings look like? It looks like a life lived as God would have us live it—in praise and appreciation!

Be blessed—and be a blessing!

Write about a time a stranger showed you kindness:

....

....

....

....

....

....

....

....

....

....

....

....

....

....

....

....

....

....

....

....

1 A shaft of sunlight breaks through a cloudy sky and you are reminded that there is always better above, always beauty to be found, and that sometimes heaven comes down to earth.

2 Another driver slows down to let you out and you realize you just encountered another soul who understands and appreciates kindness.

3 You reach out to a puppy—or a kitten, or a bird, or some other defenseless creature—and it comes to you. It's like the world just declared you a friend.

But a certain Samaritan, as he journeyed, came where he was: and when he saw him, he was moved with compassion.

LUKE 10:33 ASV

4   You grow something in the garden or in a pot that children can pick and eat. Then you remember that God did the same thing all over the world.

5   A tiny hand wraps itself around your finger and you feel depended on like never before.

6   That time you were laid low—because it gave others the chance to rise up and show, in practical ways, just how much they love you.

Write about a time you gave something only you could give:

....

....

....

....

....

....

....

....

....

....

....

....

....

....

....

....

....

....

....

....

....

....

"For they all contributed out of their abundance, but she out of her poverty has put in everything she had, all she had to live on."
MARK 12:44 ESV

Write about a time you paid a kindness forward:

....

....

....

....

....

....

....

....

....

....

....

....

....

....

....

....

....

....

....

....

7   That first cup of coffee really hits the spot and you think a moment about all the people along the production process who helped bring you that moment. Then you set out to return the favor by making the day better for someone else.

8   The Bible verse you have read a hundred times that takes on a new, deeper meaning, just when you need it most.

9   A child hands you a flower and you realize (on a level too deep for words) that innocence just handed you beauty.

And David said, "Is there still anyone left of the house of Saul,
that I may show him kindness for Jonathan's sake?"

2 SAMUEL 9:1 ESV

10 You hold a door open for someone and you give thanks for being physically able.

11 Gas prices are a worry but the stuff that fuels our bodies—a cool clear drink of water—has been around since the dawn of creation. It falls from the sky, it tumbles down mountain streams, and it won't ever run out.

12 The ability music has to peel away the worries and responsibilities of the day and take you to a place where you are as close to the pure you as it is possible to be.

Write about a particular piece of music and why it is special to you:

....
....
....
....
....
....
....
....
....
....
....
....
....
....
....
....
....
....
....
....
....
....

"Four thousand are to be gatekeepers and four thousand are to praise the Lord with the musical instruments I have provided for that purpose."
1 CHRONICLES 23:5 NIV

Write about a time you were surprised by innocence or beauty:

....

....

....

....

....

....

....

....

....

....

....

....

....

....

....

....

....

....

....

....

....

13 Birdsong captures your attention. You peer into the tree to try and identify the bird but you can't. And it doesn't matter. Because you know you don't have to see the source of your blessings to appreciate and enjoy them.

14 A child laughs with unrestrained joy and, despite your cares and responsibilities, you laugh too. Be thankful the world has a place for such pure happiness—and that it is infectious!

15 You read a journal entry you wrote so long ago you no longer remember it—but you think you would like the person who wrote it.

Let the king be enthralled by your beauty; honor him, for he is your lord.
PSALM 45:11 NIV

16 The sun. It's a massive, continuous explosion in space—but it also causes the daisy to turn toward it, ripens the harvest, and feels wonderful on your skin.

17 Waking in the morning and understanding that the new day is a chance to do more of what made your heart sing—or to change what didn't.

18 When you need a hug/someone to listen to you/good advice, and a friend turns up who just happens to be good at hugs/listening/advice. Like Someone up there knew exactly what you needed.

Write about what makes your heart sing. If you don't know, make a list and start exploring possibilities:

....

....

....

....

....

....

....

....

....

....

....

....

....

....

....

....

....

....

....

....

And David danced before the Lord with all his might;
and David was girded with a linen ephod.

2 Samuel 6:14 kjv

Write about the most precious thing you experienced this week:

....

....

....

....

....

....

....

....

....

....

....

....

....

....

....

....

....

....

19 Tears cried in sad times can actually help make you feel better. And tears cried in happy times seem to multiply the joy!

20 If you can do nothing else to help a friend, at least you can wipe a tear away. And that's no small thing in itself.

21 In a world of eight billion people, no one has the same fingerprint or retina pattern as you. You are much, much rarer than gold or diamonds!

But Mary treasured up all these things, pondering them in her heart.
LUKE 2:19 ESV

22 That place of sanctuary; the place where you can just be you with no demands on your time or your attention. Just for a little while.

23 A song on the radio speaks directly to you because the experience being sung about is yours. But it's not only yours and the singer's; it's a human experience. We all have them in common, and we are connected by them.

24 You get caught outside in a sudden rain shower. You get soaked, but you know you have clean, fresh clothes at home and a warm shower to stand in, unlike so many.

Write about what surprised you (in a nice way) about someone you thought you knew:

....

....

....

....

....

....

....

....

....

....

....

....

....

....

....

....

....

....

....

....

*Just then his disciples returned and were surprised
to find him talking with a woman. But no one asked,
"What do you want?" or "Why are you talking with her?"*

JOHN 4:27 NIV

Envisage a favorite photo from the olden days and write about what might have been happening outside the frame:

....

....

....

....

....

....

....

....

....

....

....

....

....

....

....

....

....

....

....

....

....

25 Photographs! Photos developed decades ago and kept in albums and boxes. Photos on your computer, tablet, or phone. Instant time travel. People and places from the past kept alongside us.

26 No matter what path we walk in life, there's a good chance others walked it before us, clearing obstacles as they went. Our blessing is that we, in our turn, get to make the path easier, clearer, or more beautiful for the ones who will come along after us.

27 There are always second chances in this life. We might not recognize them—but they are always there.

While he was blessing them,
he left them and was taken up into heaven.
LUKE 24:51 NIV

28 New starts. They can feel like you have nothing—or that you really have everything to gain!

29 When the new acquaintance you thought was going to be really challenging unexpectedly brings out something good in you.

30 Optimism. To those who don't have it, it's a mystery. To those who do have it, it's a mystery why everyone else doesn't!

Write about the long shot that really tested your optimism—the one no one else thought would work out but it did:

....

....

....

....

....

....

....

....

....

....

....

....

....

....

....

....

....

....

....

And Peter answered him and said, Lord, if it be thou,
bid me come unto thee upon the waters. And he said,
Come. And Peter went down from the boat, and
walked upon the waters to come to Jesus.

MATTHEW 14:28–29 ASV

Write a note of thanks to the child in your heart
for hanging on in there:

....

....

....

....

....

....

....

....

....

....

....

....

....

....

....

....

....

....

....

....

31 A child smiles and waves at you for no reason—and you remember what children still understand. We don't need a reason to reach out. We already are family!

32 A stranger you didn't realize had been watching congratulates you on some aspect of your life. It is confirmation that even when you don't think anyone sees, you are still doing the right thing. And God sees that too.

33 The opportunity to dance—with or without a partner—is nothing more than a chance to be a part of the rhythm of the universe. Go there often.

See that ye despise not one of these little ones:
for I say unto you, that in heaven their angels do always
behold the face of my Father who is in heaven.
MATTHEW 18:10 ASV

34 That person who knows your shortcomings and still loves you!

35 The healing that comes from being able to put your arms around a hurting soul...

36 ...and the comfort that comes when someone does the same to you.

Write about the time you helped someone in a way that was so simple it surprised even you:

....

....

....

....

....

....

....

....

....

....

....

....

....

....

....

....

....

....

....

....

....

....

....

....

For whosoever shall give you a cup of water to drink,
because ye are Christ's, verily I say unto you,
he shall in no wise lose his reward.

MARK 9:41 ASV

Write about the biggest difference doing the right thing has ever made to you:

....

....

....

....

....

....

....

....

....

....

....

....

....

....

....

....

....

....

37 When you find it in you to forgive someone and, in return, you discover there is more to yourself than you ever knew.

38 Your thoughts and emotions will shine through. Happiness is the cheapest beauty product there is.

39 That there is a right way in this world. Because it is often difficult and sometimes costs time, money, and effort, it doesn't really have many earthly benefits—which is why it must have come from up above.

And let us not grow weary of doing good, for in due season we will reap, if we do not give up.

GALATIANS 6:9 ESV

40 The smell of flowers is, no doubt, meant to attract bees for the pollination process. But it also lifts your heart, and you realize that God intended His creation to be more than just functional.

41 You stumble—and a hand reaches out from the crowd to steady you. It's a reminder that we are usually surrounded by good people who often only lack the opportunity to show it.

42 Laughter. You can't listen to the genuine article without being uplifted— even if you have no idea what inspired it.

Write about the time a stranger came briefly into your life and made a difference for the better:

....

....

....

....

....

....

....

....

....

....

....

....

....

....

....

....

....

....

....

....

....

Do not neglect to show hospitality to strangers,
for thereby some have entertained angels unawares.
HEBREWS 13:2 ESV

Write about a time a good thing came from a seemingly bad situation:

....

....

....

....

....

....

....

....

....

....

....

....

....

....

....

....

....

....

43 Hearts break. But hearts also heal.

44 The moment you wake up is just full of possibilities. Where will you go; who will you help smile; in what way will you grow better than you were?

45 When your temporary downturn causes an unexpected lift for someone who needs it.

"For I know the plans I have for you, declares the Lord, plans for welfare and not for evil, to give you a future and a hope."
JEREMIAH 29:11 ESV

46 We all need someone to believe in us. We don't all get that, but every one of us can be that for someone else. And in affirming them you also affirm yourself.

47 We can all be grateful for a gift, but once you understand that gratitude itself is a gift then the whole world seems wrapped in ribbons and bows.

48 Teaching children to delight in the ordinary. It reminds us that nothing is ordinary in God's creation.

Write about the person in your life who believed in you when you most needed it:

....
....
....
....
....
....
....
....
....
....
....
....
....
....
....
....
....
....
....
....

My salvation and my honor depend on God;
he is my mighty rock, my refuge.

PSALM 62:7 NIV

Write about the time one door closed and a new, surprising door opened:

....

....

....

....

....

....

....

....

....

....

....

....

....

....

....

....

....

....

....

49 How can the obstacles in your path be counted as blessings? Because they are proof positive you are moving forward.

50 The option to leave a problem that might otherwise stop you in your tracks—and to just walk around it.

51 That the choice to grow in love and to live life as it was meant to be lived is entirely up to us, and nothing in the world can change that.

"Ask and it will be given to you; seek and you will find; knock and the door will be opened to you."

MATTHEW 7:7 NIV

52 We see weeds and wildflowers growing in the most inhospitable places—through asphalt, in cracks in brick walls, on rooftops. They are a reminder that no situation is hopeless, if only we are determined to bloom.

53 The expression you wear today can make a big difference to someone's day. Choose it as carefully as you would choose your clothes. A kindly gaze or an appreciative smile is perhaps the least expensive way to do good in the world.

54 Seeing someone follow your example—whether a child or an adult, a family member or a work colleague—and seeing them be happier, healthier, more faith-filled or more successful because of it is one of the best affirmations you can ever have.

Write about someone you know who overcame a seemingly impossible situation:

....

....

....

....

....

....

....

....

....

....

....

....

....

....

....

....

....

....

....

....

....

....

....

Jesus replied, "What is impossible with man is possible with God."

LUKE 18:27 NIV

Write about a time you went against expectations and reached out to someone others might not have:

....

....

....

....

....

....

....

....

....

....

....

....

....

....

....

....

....

....

55 Being helped in some way by someone you don't get along with. A reminder that there is always more to people than whatever it is that sets them apart.

56 A fruit grows. We eat it but plant a seed. Another fruit grows, as fresh as the first. A child grows to become a parent. Then they have a child. Each generation is as wonderfully made as the last. It's evidence of eternity right in front of us—and we get to be part of it.

57 The person you never thought much of who steps forward and helps when no one else will. We are cared for from surprising directions.

And it came to pass, as he sat at meat in the house, behold, many publicans and sinners came and sat down with Jesus and his disciples.

MATTHEW 9:10 ASV

58 Memories of special days. They multiply the pleasure of those days endlessly.

59 Does your heart need you to tell it to beat? Would your hair still grow if you were to forget about it? Not everything in the world—or in your life—needs you to worry about it. Sit back once in a while. Relax. The world will still spin.

60 People die and we miss them, but babies are also born and we delight in them.

Write about what you would do if you could just take the day off from responsibility:

....

....

....

....

....

....

....

....

....

....

....

....

....

....

....

....

....

....

....

....

....

*"Come to me, all you who are weary and
burdened, and I will give you rest."*
MATTHEW 11:28 NIV

Make a list of the most valuable free things in your life:

....

....

....

....

....

....

....

....

....

....

....

....

....

....

....

....

....

....

....

....

61 In a world that seems to run on money, you don't have to look far before you realize all the things that make life worth living are free!

62 Staying in a five-star hotel is a real treat. But don't forget to look up on a clear night every once in a while. You already live in a five-billion-star "hotel."

63 The grocery bill can make quite a dent in your income. But the things that feed your soul (affirmation, encouragement…) are almost always free gifts.

Now we have received, not the spirit of the world, but the spirit which is of God; that we might know the things that are freely given to us of God.

1 CORINTHIANS 2:12 KJV

64 The inquiring minds of children will teach us what we don't know, and explaining things to them will deepen our understanding.

65 You get the chance to rescue an injured bird or small creature. You have just become proof that in a harsh and often cruel world, there is also help from unexpected quarters.

66 The answer to most of the problems in the world is more love. And you have an endless ability to produce more love.

Write about something that time spent with a child reminded you of:

....
....
....
....
....
....
....
....
....
....
....
....
....
....
....
....
....
....
....
....

And he said: "Truly I tell you, unless you change and become like little children, you will never enter the kingdom of heaven."

MATTHEW 18:3 NIV

Write about how you made the world a happier place today (or this week):

....
....
....
....
....
....
....
....
....
....
....
....
....
....
....
....
....
....
....

67 You have it in you to raise the happiness total of the whole world by making just one person smile. (And you don't have to stop there!)

68 You don't have to be a farmer to plant seeds that will turn into a wonderful crop.

69 A little change of attitude can turn an ordeal into an adventure!

And they offered great sacrifices that day, and rejoiced; for God had made them rejoice with great joy; and the women also and the children rejoiced: so that the joy of Jerusalem was heard even afar off.

NEHEMIAH 12:43 ASV

70 Almost everyone you have ever met has been a teacher in one way or another.

71 Today is not yesterday. And that's a much bigger blessing than it might seem!

72 If you are interested in people, you find you are surrounded by interesting people.

Write about a value you encouraged in someone that you saw blossom later:

....

....

....

....

....

....

....

....

....

....

....

....

....

....

....

....

....

....

....

....

Therefore encourage one another and build each other up, just as in fact you are doing.
1 THESSALONIANS 5:11 NIV

Write a short list of things you depend on daily that were made or operated by people you have never met:

....
....
....
....
....
....
....

73 Every person you meet was once a child. You have that in common with them.

74 You are surrounded by examples of work people did to the best of their ability, enabling you to rely on it.

75 Isn't it wonderful that things that grow in the ground, apparently without any direction, just happen to have all the vitamins and nutrients that we need?

And they spake unto Moses, saying, The people bring much more than enough for the service of the work which Jehovah commanded to make.

EXODUS 36:5 ASV

76 The internet takes away the difficulties of distance and allows you to have friends all over the world.

77 Work may be a grind—but millions of people would love to have your job.

78 Memories of loved ones are more than simply memories—they are encouragers, teachers, examples, and a refuge in troubled times.

Make a list of your farthest away friends and how you keep in touch with them:

....

....

....

....

....

....

....

....

....

....

....

....

....

....

....

....

....

....

....

....

....

*And he said unto them, Go ye into all the world,
and preach the gospel to the whole creation.*

MARK 16:15 ASV

Is there anyone you know who might be lonely and would appreciate a little conversation? Write a few words on how you would do that:

....

....

....

....

....

....

....

....

....

....

....

....

....

....

....

....

79 Imagine there was no sense of taste. How much poorer would your world be for that lack? If you can taste things, then savor and celebrate that ability.

80 That feeling when you stand on the grass or the dirt with your bare feet and you feel connected to something.

81 Animals manage to fight or be friendly without the ability to communicate through speech. We have the ability to talk. Let's do something more with it.

"Go and stand in the temple and speak to the people all the words of this Life."

ACTS 5:20 ESV

82 A tire swing! It's not a blessing in itself, but the chance to do something innocent, silly, and childlike when you are an adult certainly is!

83 In every good book is a new world someone created for you to share.

84 Being secure enough that you can switch your mind off for eight hours every night.

Write about the most fun place you ever slept as a child:

....

....

....

....

....

....

....

....

....

....

....

....

....

....

....

....

....

....

....

*And he came to a certain place and stayed there that night,
because the sun had set. Taking one of the stones of the place,
he put it under his head and lay down in that place to sleep.*

GENESIS 28:11 ESV

Make a list of skills you would like to learn:

....

....

....

....

....

....

....

....

....

....

....

....

....

....

....

....

....

....

85   Did you ever learn a new skill that made your life worse? No. So keep on learning new skills!

86   Keeping a plant in your home and watching it grow is a reminder that things will unfold the way they are supposed to (without worrying).

87   If you get the chance to be silly, take it and enjoy it. It means you are safe and secure and probably in the company of friends who will take care of the sensible things—at least for a little while.

"He has filled them with skill to do all kinds of work as engravers, designers, embroiderers in blue, purple and scarlet yarn and fine linen, and weavers—all of them skilled workers and designers."
EXODUS 35:35 NIV

88 Making someone laugh is a wonderful gift. It means that, even if only for a moment, you lifted them out of all their worries and took them to a kinder place.

89 When a friend reaches out to you for help. It may cost you time, money, or effort, but you will have been blessed by the asking.

90 The candle might be small and its flame easily blown out, but while it burns it has the ability to shut out the wider world and bring you into the here and now.

Write about how you center yourself when it seems the world wants to pull you in twenty different directions:

....

....

....

....

....

....

....

....

....

....

....

....

....

....

....

....

....

....

....

He says, "Be still, and know that I am God; I will be exalted among the nations, I will be exalted in the earth."
PSALM 46:10 NIV

Make a short list of things you could make more beautiful through a little of your time and effort:

....

....

....

....

....

....

....

....

....

....

....

....

....

....

....

....

....

91 A walk in the park might seem like nothing much, but at some point someone bought that land, or laid it aside, for everyone to enjoy. Thank them, retroactively, by enjoying it a little more.

92 The ability to look on the bright side is a gift.

93 There is an innate beauty in every living thing. With a little practice you will end up seeing beauty wherever you go.

Your beauty should not come from outward adornment, such as elaborate hairstyles and the wearing of gold jewelry or fine clothes. Rather, it should be that of your inner self, the unfading beauty of a gentle and quiet spirit, which is of great worth in God's sight.

1 PETER 3:3–4 NIV

94 Children, whether yours or other people's, are proof that there will be a future.

95 Being involved in the lives of children allows you to play a part in shaping the future.

96 Epiphanies. Those moments when everything makes sense. Those have to be gifts!

✳

Write about a time you spoke words of encouragement to a dispirited child:

....

....

....

....

....

....

....

....

....

....

....

....

....

....

....

....

....

....

....

....

And taking the child by the hand, he saith unto her, Talitha cumi;
which is, being interpreted, Damsel, I say unto thee, Arise.

MARK 5:41 ASV

Write about a time your effort to help snowballed, becoming more than you could have expected:

....

....

....

....

....

....

....

....

....

....

....

....

....

....

....

....

....

....

....

97 The moon. As well as being romantic, it is a night-light for the whole world. How convenient (or how well arranged).

98 When you give something to help someone and discover they shared it with someone else in need. Enabling someone else to be kind might just be worth more than the actual gift.

99 If you have someone in this world who puts you first and whom you can rely on absolutely, you have a little glimpse of what it is like to be loved from above.

Do ye not yet perceive, neither remember the five loaves of the five thousand, and how many baskets ye took up?
MATTHEW 16:9 ASV

100 Friends aren't just something you make at school and keep forever. Each new day brings the chance to find another old-friend-in-the-making.

101 There are aspects of our personalities that are deeper than skin-deep and aren't easy to see—which is why we have jewelry, shoes, and our own style in clothes.

102 Not all our thoughts show in our expressions, which is a good thing. It gives us time to work on having the kind of thoughts we would be happy to wear on our faces.

Write about your style in life, what makes you distinctively you:

....
....
....
....
....
....
....
....
....
....
....
....
....
....
....
....
....
....
....
....

*I will praise thee; for I am fearfully and wonderfully made:
marvellous are thy works; and that my soul knoweth right well.*

PSALM 139:14 KJV

Compile a list of the blessings you normally take
for granted—and work on appreciating them more:

....

....

....

....

....

....

....

....

....

....

....

....

....

....

....

....

....

....

103 Someone holds a door open for you and you see it as a gift of grace—which you also, through God's blessing, have been able to share with others.

104 Pets never judge you. (Unless they are cats, and they can usually be bribed.)

105 We surround our birthdays with ideas of parties, gifts, or getting older. Let's not forget that it's a day people celebrate our arrival in the world too.

*And God is able to bless you abundantly, so that in all things at all times,
having all that you need, you will abound in every good work.*

2 CORINTHIANS 9:8 NIV

106 The world never runs short of little girls and little boys, and that's a good thing because we need to be reminded of innocence and joy.

107 The friend who has seen you at your worst and at your best but only ever mentions the latter.

108 Uncommon colors, like vermilion, damask, and jasper. They remind us that life is more subtly beautiful than it first seems.

Write a thank-you note to your oldest friend:

Greet Rufus, chosen in the Lord; also his mother,
who has been a mother to me as well.
ROMANS 16:13 ESV

Write about the most enjoyable surprise you ever prepared:

....

....

....

....

....

....

....

....

....

....

....

....

....

....

....

....

....

....

....

....

109 Keeping a secret to surprise someone. Not only does it exercise our patience, but it also lets us enjoy the moment long before it ever happens.

110 Libraries. Why? As many reasons as there are books on the shelves.

111 "Difficult" people. They give us opportunities for us to grow—and to teach.

*"You should not be surprised at my saying,
'You must be born again.'"*

JOHN 3:7 NIV

112 Tokens of encouragement from strangers who know you are having a difficult time can seem like they were delivered by angels.

113 The fact that kittens and puppies chase their own tails would seem to be proof that God has a sense of humor and that life is meant to be enjoyed.

114 Change is always an option. Use it to make things better.

Write about the most unusual way you were ever encouraged:

....
....
....
....
....
....
....
....
....
....
....
....
....
....
....
....
....
....
....
....
....

"Lord," she replied, "even the dogs under the table eat the children's crumbs." Then he told her, "For such a reply, you may go; the demon has left your daughter."

MARK 7:28–29 NIV

Write about the person, not related to you, who is most like family and how that came to be:

....

....

....

....

....

....

....

....

....

....

....

....

....

....

....

....

....

....

....

115 Having someone hold your hand, or having someone's hand to hold.

116 The fact that family doesn't have to share the same DNA (except from way, way, way back).

117 That when it seems you have nothing, hope is still a very real thing.

When Jesus therefore saw his mother, and the disciple standing by, whom he loved, he saith unto his mother, Woman, behold thy son!
JOHN 19:26 KJV

118 The fact that there are people willing to give up home comforts and travel across the world just to help others who never had those home comforts.

119 Chatting via email or text messaging has its limitations, but it does allow heart-to-heart conversations without appearance or culture getting in the way.

120 A friend who will do what they can for you in difficult times and still be there even when there is nothing else they can do for you is a very great blessing indeed.

If you could be a missionary for a cause, what would it be and what would you do?

....

....

....

....

....

....

....

....

....

....

....

....

....

....

....

....

....

....

....

The woman then left her waterpot, and went her way into the city, and saith to the men, Come, see a man, which told me all things that ever I did: is not this the Christ?

JOHN 4:28–29 KJV

Write about the person you always turn to for help and how you could show your appreciation:

....
....
....
....
....
....
....
....
....
....
....
....
....
....
....
....
....
....
....
....
....

121   A friend you can always turn to if you need anything is a blessing. If you are that friend to others, then you are the blessing—which is, in itself, a blessing!

122   A friend who always keeps their promise is usually true to a higher set of values and they are worth keeping around.

123   You do someone an "ordinary" kindness, only to discover no one has ever done that for them before. Your ordinary kindness just became extraordinary.

And [she] stood at his feet behind him weeping, and began to wash his feet with tears, and did wipe them with the hairs of her head, and kissed his feet, and anointed them with the ointment.

LUKE 7:38 KJV

124 The words you speak can change how you feel—if you have it in your heart to speak those words.

125 Smiling when you don't feel like smiling—will make you feel like smiling!

126 A stream that flows strongly is usually clean and life-giving. Allow good things like kindness, love, sharing, empathy, and sacrifice to flow through your life and you will be like that stream.

Write about a time you were feeling low and you encouraged yourself out of it:

....

....

....

....

....

....

....

....

....

....

....

....

....

....

....

....

....

....

....

And he went forward a little, and fell on his face, and prayed, saying, My Father, if it be possible, let this cup pass away from me: nevertheless, not as I will, but as thou wilt.

MATTHEW 26:39 ASV

Choose a piece of music, architecture, or particular food from elsewhere in the world that inspires a sense of awe and wonder in you. Try to find the words to describe it:

....

....

....

....

....

....

....

....

....

....

....

....

....

....

....

....

....

127 Orchestras prove that we don't all have to be the same to work in harmony and make beautiful music.

128 We are blessed to be able to enjoy foods from all over the world—often made locally!

129 A sense of wonder!

God saw all that he had made, and it was very good.
And there was evening, and there was morning—the sixth day.
GENESIS 1:31 NIV

130 The way the sound of a gurgling stream can wash our concerns away.

131 Singing—it's an outlet for the soul.

132 Tears, and the way enough of them can leave you feeling better even though the situation causing them hasn't changed.

Write about your favorite natural therapy:

....
....
....
....
....
....
....
....
....
....
....
....
....
....
....
....
....
....
....
....
....
....

When he had thus spoken, he spat on the ground, and made clay of the spittle, and anointed his eyes with the clay.

JOHN 9:6 ASV

Write about your best winter day ever:

....
....
....
....
....
....
....
....
....
....
....
....
....
....
....
....
....
....
....
....
....
....

133 Snuggling in.

134 Firsts that show progress: first word, first kiss, first dance…

135 Summer days and winter days and what the experience of each one brings to the enjoyment of the other.

For everything there is a season,
and a time for every matter under heaven.
ECCLESIASTES 3:1 ESV

136 The world in all its wonderful variety could never be properly explored in one lifetime—but you could try!

137 Finding a pretty or peaceful corner of your hometown or city you never knew existed.

138 The friend whose friendship doesn't depend on shared experiences or common interests. You just like them and they like you.

Write about your favorite travel destination, in actuality or in your dreams:

....

....

....

....

....

....

....

....

....

....

....

....

....

....

....

....

....

....

....

Hear, Israel, and be careful to obey so that it may go well with you and that you may increase greatly in a land flowing with milk and honey, just as the LORD, the God of your ancestors, promised you.

DEUTERONOMY 6:3 NIV

Write about the last time you were compelled to do nothing:

....
....
....
....
....
....
....
....
....
....
....
....
....
....
....
....
....
....
....
....

139 When a child falls asleep on your lap, and you dare not move and there is no TV to watch or music to listen to, so you just have to savor the moment, and the next moment, and the next....

140 Something falling apart always leaves space for a new thing to grow.

141 A family gathered around the dinner table who appreciates the meal but looks more at each other than the dinner.

And Jesus answered and said unto her, Martha, Martha, thou art careful and troubled about many things: but one thing is needful: and Mary hath chosen that good part, which shall not be taken away from her.

LUKE 10:41–42 KJV

142 Furniture from a bygone era that still has the feel of its original owners about it.

143 Sloping floors and low ceilings in old buildings. Reminders that, even when things weren't perfect, people still lived their lives.

144 The feeling of "family" that emanates from a kitchen well used.

Write about your favorite "imperfect" object:

....

....

....

....

....

....

....

....

....

....

....

....

....

....

....

....

....

....

....

....

....

....

For we know in part and we prophesy in part,
but when completeness comes, what is in part disappears.
1 CORINTHIANS 13:9–10 NIV

List the good things about growing older (and ignore the other stuff):

....

....

....

....

....

....

....

....

....

....

....

....

....

....

....

....

....

....

....

....

145 The fact that, against all expectation, some things (and people) do get better with age.

146 Beautiful views belong to everyone.

147 Having a passion or interest that is outside day-to-day survival—and being able to indulge in it.

"Even to your old age and gray hairs I am he, I am he who will sustain you. I have made you and I will carry you; I will sustain you and I will rescue you."

ISAIAH 46:4 NIV

148 The ability to shrug and say, "Oh well," when things don't turn out quite how you planned.

149 The opportunity to saunter, anywhere, is a much underrated blessing.

150 Those moments when we lose all control. Because they allow more opportunities for God to work in our lives.

Write about a time your plans went awry—with good results:

....

....

....

....

....

....

....

....

....

....

....

....

....

....

....

....

....

....

....

Commit your work to the LORD,
and your plans will be established.
PROVERBS 16:3 ESV

Write about the last really good night's sleep you had (or the next one you plan to have):

....

....

....

....

....

....

....

....

....

....

....

....

....

....

....

....

....

....

151 Preparing a hot meal for those out working in the cold. It's a double thank-you. You are appreciating their work and appreciating the fact that you don't have to go out in the cold.

152 The times when you get carried away over your enthusiasm for something. It's nice to be reminded that the uninhibited child is still in there.

153 That time between full sleep and full wakefulness. Especially if you are sharing it with a loved one.

Then Jacob awoke from his sleep and said,
"Surely the Lord is in this place, and I did not know it."
GENESIS 28:16 ESV

154 Lasting virtues and forever truths in a constantly changing world.

155 Having beautiful ornaments in your house and appreciating them not just for themselves but for the time, skill, and care that went into producing them. In caring for them you become a custodian of beauty.

156 Someone who might not be able to solve your problems but will happily face them all right alongside you.

Write about the most beautiful object you possess—and why it holds that place in your appreciation:

....
....
....
....
....
....
....
....
....
....
....
....
....
....
....
....
....
....
....

But you are a chosen people, a royal priesthood, a holy nation, God's special possession, that you may declare the praises of him who called you out of darkness into his wonderful light.

1 PETER 2:9 NIV

Write about the last little kindness someone you don't really know well did for you:

....

....

....

....

....

....

....

....

....

....

....

....

....

....

....

....

....

....

....

157   Gratitude is a blessing that grows. The more you are grateful for, the more you see to be grateful for.

158   When someone, whether a family member or a server in a café, just gets the mood you are in and does some little thing to enhance it.

159   Rainbows. The sky might be lighter inside the rainbow, but the colors are most intense against the dark side. Be a rainbow, and be more brilliant in darker times.

A man with leprosy came and knelt before him and said,
"Lord, if you are willing, you can make me clean." Jesus reached
out his hand and touched the man "I am willing," he said
"Be clean!" Immediately he was cleansed of his leprosy.

Matthew 8:2–3 NIV

160 Contentment. It's a fleeting butterfly of an emotion, but when it lands on you there is nothing to compare with it.

161 Outdoor fountains on a sunny day. Only some reckless children may kick off their shoes and go splashing—but everyone wants to!

162 Trees that give shade and shelter even to those who didn't plant them.

Write about the last time you felt truly content:

....

....

....

....

....

....

....

....

....

....

....

....

....

....

....

....

....

....

....

....

....

....

Now may the Lord of peace himself give you peace at all times and in every way. The Lord be with all of you.
2 THESSALONIANS 3:16 NIV

Write about your favorite childhood walk:

....

....

....

....

....

....

....

....

....

....

....

....

....

....

....

....

....

163 Seeing your parents happy and realizing that, as their child, you probably played a big part in their happiness.

164 When someone says "Forget it"—and really means it!

165 A good walk when things are overwhelming not only physically takes you away from the problems, but it also reminds you that there is so much more to life.

That very day two of them were going to a village named Emmaus, about seven miles from Jerusalem, and they were talking with each other about all these things that had happened. While they were talking and discussing together, Jesus himself drew near and went with them.

LUKE 24:13–15 ESV

166 Simple tasks like straightening a rug, or tidying your shoes, or fixing your hair as a reminder that you can bring a little order to what sometimes seems like a chaotic world. And even if no one else knows it, you do!

167 The sun has never yet failed to rise in the morning, even after the longest nights.

168 Getting the chance to do something with your father that he likes. It's his payback for all the childish things he probably didn't want to do—but did!

Write about a time you were able to give something back:

....
....
....
....
....
....
....
....
....
....
....
....
....
....
....
....
....
....
....

Then took Mary a pound of ointment of spikenard, very costly, and anointed the feet of Jesus, and wiped his feet with her hair: and the house was filled with the odour of the ointment.

JOHN 12:3 KJV

Write a thank-you letter to the person who most helped to shape your values:

....

....

....

....

....

....

....

....

....

....

....

....

....

....

....

....

....

....

....

169 Having a past you can look back on with pleasure.

170 The knowledge that you are better prepared now than you ever have been, so what comes next will surely be better than what went before.

171 When someone can tell by the gift or the action that you were the giver or the doer. (Especially when the gift is considered a thoughtful one and the action is considered kind.)

I always thank my God for you because of his grace given you in Christ Jesus.

1 CORINTHIANS 1:4 NIV

172 Finding things like beach pebbles and buttonhooks that you have no use for but you can't ignore their intrinsic beauty.

173 Anticipation, whether justified or not, is a pleasure in its own right.

174 Unexpectedly seeing a wild animal in its natural environment—and not on the road in front of you.

Write about your favorite experience in the wild:

....

....

....

....

....

....

....

....

....

....

....

....

....

....

....

....

....

....

....

....

*And so John the Baptist appeared in the wilderness,
preaching a baptism of repentance for the forgiveness of sins.*

MARK 1:4 NIV

Write about the last time you cast inhibitions to the wind:

....

....

....

....

....

....

....

....

....

....

....

....

....

....

....

....

....

....

....

175 The feeling that comes with mastering a new skill. It's like being the child who finally learned to tie their shoelaces.

176 The way writing a problem or an idea down on paper automatically frees space in your head.

177 Children's parties where you are compelled to behave foolishly. It's like temporarily setting your heart free.

*I will walk about in freedom,
for I have sought out your precepts.*
PSALM 119:45 NIV

178 Finally understanding that great truths are never complex. Their unexpected simplicity is why they so often go untried.

179 Trying one of those great truths.

180 Realizing that your ordinary life is only ordinary to you. To others it would make a fascinating book (as their lives might to you).

Write about a time you took a moral stance:

....

....

....

....

....

....

....

....

....

....

....

....

....

....

....

....

....

....

....

....

....

*Because of my integrity you uphold
me and set me in your presence forever.*

PSALM 41:12 NIV

Compile a list of your favorite old-fashioned words:

....

....

....

....

....

....

....

....

....

....

....

....

....

....

....

....

....

....

181 That moment in the evening when you stop to realize it has been a good day.

182 When the winter bedding comes out. (Also, the fact that you have winter bedding.)

183 Discovering an old-fashioned word for a concept that has gone out of fashion and realizing that the world wasn't always seen the way we see it now.

In the beginning was the Word, and the Word was with God, and the Word was God.
JOHN 1:1 ASV

184 The people who will step forward and invest time and effort in the local community.

185 Helping those people in some small way, even if it is only buying cakes from their bake sale. You are still playing an essential part.

186 When the answer to a long-running dilemma just pops into your head. Either you figured it out for yourself, which is great, or it was a gift from above, which is greater.

Write about someone you consider to be a local hero:

....
....
....
....
....
....
....
....
....
....
....
....
....
....
....
....
....

And they said, Cornelius a centurion, a righteous man and one that feareth God, and well reported of by all the nation of the Jews, was warned of God by a holy angel to send for thee into his house, and to hear words from thee.

Acts 10:22 ASV

Write about waiting for *that* invitation and *that* dance:

....

....

....

....

....

....

....

....

....

....

....

....

....

....

....

....

....

....

187   Being asked to dance.

188   Making up with someone you fell out with. That's when you realize that friendship is more important than the things that often break it.

189   The shortest day of the year. Because the next day there will be more sunshine. And the next. And the next. And…

"Blessed is the one who listens to me, watching daily at my gates, waiting beside my doors."

PROVERBS 8:34 ESV

190 The imagination of children begs a very important question. After all, they have hardly had time to develop something so wondrous. Neither have they learned our self-imposed limitations. So. . .maybe the world is really supposed to be like that!

191 Saying grace before meals, if it is not a formulaic thing, is a three times daily reminder of what we have to be thankful for.

192 When someone says "No problem" after doing you a favor and you realize it was more than no problem. They actually delighted in helping you.

Write about letting someone help because of how much it meant to them:

....
....
....
....
....
....
....
....
....
....
....
....
....
....
....
....
....
....
....
....

He brought me out into a spacious place;
he rescued me because he delighted in me.
PSALM 18:19 NIV

Write about the most interesting detour or wrong turn you ever took:

....

....

....

....

....

....

....

....

....

....

....

....

....

....

....

....

....

....

....

193 Drawing a line through that final item on your to-do list.

194 Drawing a line through that first item on your to-do list. Starting off with a success encourages you to look at the other things on the list and say, "I can do this!"

195 Wynds. Paths that follow the contours of the land or the less dense areas of the wood. A reminder that getting there quickly isn't always the most important thing.

"I have led you forty years in the wilderness. Your clothes have not worn out on you, and your sandals have not worn off your feet."

DEUTERONOMY 29:5 ESV

196 A spectacular sunset. Not just for the enjoyment of it, but because most days the sun goes down unnoticed. It's a reminder that, even though many of our days are ordinary, we too can still be spectacular from time to time.

197 The thorn in your side—the difficulty or regret that stays with you, but the overcoming of which makes you a better person.

198 Having good neighbors—or even one good neighbor—is a much underrated blessing.

What has been your greatest personal struggle?

....
....
....
....
....
....
....
....
....
....
....
....
....
....
....
....
....
....
....
....
....

And being in an agony he prayed more earnestly;
and his sweat became as it were great drops
of blood falling down upon the ground.
LUKE 22:44 ASV

Write about that time (or your favorite time) when your kindness was unexpectedly rewarded:

....

....

....

....

....

....

....

....

....

....

....

....

....

....

....

....

....

199   The opportunity to be a good neighbor.

200   The fact that there is always a deeper understanding to be had— of everything!

201   The fact that if you give, you shall receive.

Jesus answered and said unto her, If thou knewest the gift of God, and who it is that saith to thee, Give me to drink; thou wouldest have asked of him, and he would have given thee living water.

JOHN 4:10 ASV

202 The fact that broken hearts do heal and the pain you thought would sweep you away is eventually all but forgotten. There is healing.

203 The unexpected exercise that makes you breathe deeply and causes your heart to jump. It's a reminder of how much you are capable of physically and how wonderfully you have been made.

204 The fact that love isn't easy—which makes it all the more precious.

Write about the greatest risk you ever took for love (any kind of love):

....

....

....

....

....

....

....

....

....

....

....

....

....

....

....

....

....

"Wash, put on perfume, and get dressed in your best clothes. Then go down to the threshing floor, but don't let him know you are there until he has finished eating and drinking. When he lies down, note the place where he is lying. Then go and uncover his feet and lie down. He will tell you what to do."

RUTH 3:3–4 NIV

Write about how you think others see you:

....

....

....

....

....

....

....

....

....

....

205 Being known for something nice.

206 Not being known for something nasty (which is almost as important).

207 The fact that the world spins and tilts, giving us days, nights, and seasons—and yet it still stays in perfect orbit.

....

....

....

....

....

....

....

....

....

....

....

....

....

For we are his workmanship, created in Christ Jesus for good works,
which God afore prepared that we should walk in them.

EPHESIANS 2:10 ASV

208 The smile that means something special only to you and one other person.

209 Butterflies—a sign that ordinary life will be followed by something much more spectacular.

210 The hardy "wagoneers" who made the trails that became our interstates.

Write a short letter to someone you miss:

....

....

....

....

....

....

....

....

....

....

....

....

....

....

....

....

....

....

....

....

....

....

I thank my God every time I remember you. In all my prayers for all of you, I always pray with joy.

PHILIPPIANS 1:3–4 NIV

Write about the most unusual—or most unexpected—compliment you ever received:

....

....

....

....

....

....

....

....

....

....

....

....

....

....

....

....

....

....

....

....

211   That we all have a guiding voice that knows the right thing to do (whether we listen or not).

212   A compliment from someone we know has no ulterior motive.

213   There might be hundreds of different languages in the world, but they all translate into the same images in the mind and the same emotions in the heart.

"You are the light of the world. A town built on a hill cannot be hidden."

Matthew 5:14 NIV

214 If you smile at someone, there is a good chance they will smile back, and you get to improve two people's days for the price of one smile.

215 Having had a childhood worth keeping around to help guide you through your adulthood.

216 Ribbons and lace edges where they aren't strictly necessary. Because something in us expects life to be more than simply what is strictly necessary.

Do you remember the most beautifully presented gift you ever received?

....

....

....

....

....

....

....

....

....

....

....

....

....

....

....

....

....

....

....

....

Every good gift and every perfect gift is from above, coming down from the Father of lights, with whom can be no variation, neither shadow that is cast by turning.

JAMES 1:17 ASV

If you did ever manage to complete that journal of your life, what would the movie be called and who would play you?

....
....
....
....
....
....
....
....
....
....
....
....
....
....
....
....
....
....
....
....

217 People worth aspiring to be like, either from history or currently in your life.

218 The way sunlight gets absorbed by wood and can be released again as flames. (The same applies to coal and oil, but you can't beat sitting by a crackling wood fire.)

219 The possibilities in a new notebook or diary. (Hoping to fill it with wonderful stuff—but generally forgetting!)

I have fought the good fight, I have finished the race, I have kept the faith.

2 TIMOTHY 4:7 NIV

220 Delicious recipes—and the people who first thought, *Let's add a little...*

221 Individual snowflakes. If you want to convince anyone that this universe was made, and not by accident, show them a magnified picture of a snowflake. (As well as making a convincing argument that they are also beautiful!)

222 The weather. It's something you will have in common with everyone you meet and a great conversation starter.

Some foods seem to go better with certain special occasions. Make a list of favorite foods and the events you associate them with. Avoid the obvious ones and keep it personal:

....

....

....

....

....

....

....

....

....

....

....

....

....

....

....

....

....

*And the house of Israel called the name thereof Manna:
and it was like coriander seed, white; and the taste
of it was like wafers made with honey.*

EXODUS 16:31 ASV

Write about someone in your life who provided strong walls when you needed shelter:

....

....

....

....

....

....

....

....

....

....

....

....

....

....

....

....

....

....

....

....

....

223 Picturesque harbors. Why shouldn't they be picturesque? Protection from the storms of life is a beautiful thing.

224 The One who is a safe harbor for you.

225 The one (or ones) you shelter and keep safe.

For he will hide me in his shelter in the day of trouble; he will conceal me under the cover of his tent; he will lift me high upon a rock.

PSALM 27:5 ESV

226 Green shoots poking through the covering of last year's leaves. A reminder that there is a time to nurture and a time to grow.

227 The fact that growth gives purpose to nurturing and nurturing makes growth possible. (And that life was arranged to be so interdependent.)

228 The way that most weeds, in the right place, are actually wildflowers.

Write about someone you know who didn't fit in, until they (hopefully) found the right place to grow:

....

....

....

....

....

....

....

....

....

....

....

....

....

....

....

....

....

....

*Now when he rose early on the first day of the week,
he appeared first to Mary Magdalene, from whom
he had cast out seven demons.*

MARK 16:9 ESV

What do you know now that would have amazed thirteen-year-old you?

....

....

....

....

....

....

....

....

....

....

....

....

....

....

....

....

....

....

229 Look beyond the grocery shopping and the tidying up after the meal every once in a while and think about what a blessing it is to be able to feed those you love.

230 That life continues to be wonderful even after each age your younger self was sure signified the end.

231 The way some things "mysteriously" work out just right.

When I was a child, I spake as a child, I understood as a child, I thought as a child: but when I became a man, I put away childish things.

1 CORINTHIANS 13:11 KJV

232 Your hair and the comfort it brings to both of you when a child plays with it.

233 The opportunities to build your life in imaginative play as a child before you have to do it for real as an adult.

234 The fact that so many wise men and women really thought about life and left their thoughts for us to read, ignore, or explore.

What were your favorite games as a child? How do those games still play out in your life?

....
....
....
....
....
....
....
....
....
....
....
....
....
....
....
....
....
....
....
....

Everyone who competes in the games goes into strict training. They do it to get a crown that will not last, but we do it to get a crown that will last forever.

1 CORINTHIANS 9:25 NIV

What bargain are you proudest of, and which has given you the greatest return for your money?

....

....

....

....

....

....

....

....

....

....

....

....

....

....

....

....

....

....

....

....

235 That, when tested, you have more strength and perseverance than you ever thought you had.

236 Getting a bargain (and knowing that the seller still made a profit, even if it wasn't as big a profit as they were aiming for).

237 The opportunity to adopt or sponsor someone in difficult circumstances. Often you are rescuing (or saving) a life.

"It is like a mustard seed, which a man took and planted in his garden. It grew and became a tree, and the birds perched in its branches."

LUKE 13:19 NIV

238 Forgiveness. There is no reason it should exist in a world that wasn't governed by love—but it does.

239 Encouraging someone to try again. (And the difficulty you had to overcome so you would know that trying again is worth it.)

240 Opportunities to show others that they are loved. (And the fact that the sun hasn't yet risen on a day when there wasn't at least an opportunity to do that.)

Write about a time you reached out to someone who seemed, in one way or another, isolated:

....

....

....

....

....

....

....

....

....

....

....

....

....

....

....

....

....

....

....

....

*Then was brought unto him one possessed with
a demon, blind and dumb: and he healed him,
insomuch that the dumb man spake and saw.*

MATTHEW 12:22 ASV

Write about a creative solution to a problem that you came up with (or the one someone else came up with that impressed you the most):

....

....

....

....

....

....

....

....

....

....

....

....

....

....

....

....

241 The ingenuity that enables people to adapt and thrive in many different circumstances. We are an amazing species!

242 Those precious times when you can get away from it all, whether it be a vacation or simply sitting in the backyard after dark when no one knows you are there.

243 Having someone—or something—to come home to.

And when they could not get near him because of the crowd, they removed the roof above him, and when they had made an opening, they let down the bed on which the paralytic lay.

MARK 2:4 ESV

244 Habits—if they are good, life-affirming ones. In fact, being life-affirming is a fine habit to get into in itself!

245 Habits that aren't good and life-affirming. It's important to have something to overcome in your life.

246 Making future "good old days" today.

Think of something you could do tomorrow (or soon) that could go on to become a special memory for someone:

....

....

....

....

....

....

....

....

....

....

....

....

....

....

....

....

....

I think it is right to refresh your memory as long as I live in the tent of this body, because I know that I will soon put it aside, as our Lord Jesus Christ has made clear to me. And I will make every effort to see that after my departure you will always be able to remember these things.

2 PETER 1:13–15 NIV

Write about: a situation that anyone could have made better—but you were the one who did! Even if it was only a little thing.

247 Understanding that in all the important ways your life is much like that of every person who ever lived.

248 Individuality. There are seven billion people on the planet right now, and you are the only one who is you.

249 The knowledge that you can always make a situation a little better, somehow or other.

Religion that God our Father accepts as pure and faultless is this: to look after orphans and widows in their distress and to keep oneself from being polluted by the world.

JAMES 1:27 NIV

250 Achievements, big and small. (It's not really about the achievement; it's about the self-belief you take from it to the next task.)

251 When what you feared doesn't happen. Who took care of that?

252 Having someone depend on you. It's only a worry if you don't think you're dependable—but they obviously do!

Have you ever had to deal with a child's irrational fear? What creative solution did you come up with?

....

....

....

....

....

....

....

....

....

....

....

....

....

....

....

....

....

....

....

....

....

*For I, Jehovah thy God, will hold thy right hand,
saying unto thee, Fear not; I will help thee.*
ISAIAH 41:13 ASV

Write a short poem dedicated to hugs. (But best stick to describing the feelings and avoid the actual word. You don't want to end up rhyming with *bugs*):

....

....

....

....

....

....

....

....

....

....

....

....

....

....

....

....

....

....

253 A warm hug on a cold day.

254 Any kind of hug on any kind of day.

255 Knowing you're home for the night after a tough day. PJs, slippers, a hot drink, and your favorite drama on TV.

But Esau ran to meet him and embraced him and fell on his neck and kissed him, and they wept.

GENESIS 33:4 ESV

256 The fact that there are still some people prepared to risk the ridicule of the world to stand up for something good.

257 Being one of those people.

258 Different cultures. A reminder that there are many ways to do life.

❄

Write a list of the foods, drinks, traditions, and so on that have enriched our culture but started off elsewhere in the world:

....

....

....

....

....

....

....

....

....

....

....

....

....

....

....

....

....

....

....

Now the LORD had said unto Abram, Get thee out of thy country, and from thy kindred, and from thy father's house, unto a land that I will shew thee.

GENESIS 12:1 KJV

Write a thank-you letter to someone who gave you a boost up the ladder of life in some way. Tell them the good that came from their kindness:

....

....

....

....

....

....

....

....

....

....

....

....

....

....

....

....

....

259 Days when the weather means you can't go anywhere—so you get to stay at home and appreciate what you have.

260 Getting the chance to help someone who is actively trying to better their situation.

261 Having someone help when you are actively trying to better your situation.

Greet Priscilla and Aquila, my co-workers in Christ Jesus. They risked their lives for me. Not only I but all the churches of the Gentiles are grateful to them.

ROMANS 16:3–4 NIV

262 Having friends who are willing—or eager—to do something silly with you. (And at least one friend who is sensible enough to say, okay, that's just too silly.)

263 That your circumstances have no control over your dreams but your dreams can change your circumstances.

264 Being a part of the Milky Way, not just a spectator on a clear night.

Write about your role in your circle of friends. What part do you play?

....

....

....

....

....

....

....

....

....

....

....

....

....

....

....

....

....

....

Thus Joseph, who was also called by the apostles Barnabas (which means son of encouragement), a Levite, a native of Cyprus, sold a field that belonged to him and brought the money and laid it at the apostles' feet.

ACTS 4:36–37 ESV

Make a list of where your favorite foods actually come from, and ask God to bless those involved in bringing food to your table:

....

....

....

....

....

....

....

....

....

....

....

....

....

....

....

....

....

....

....

265 The many worlds that books and imagination can transport you to.

266 Visiting some wilderness with a camera or sketch pad, intent on taking some of it back with you. (But of course you take it back, primarily, in your heart.)

267 Watching the fishing boats come in or the harvesters in the fields and giving thanks for the people who really stock the supermarket shelves.

As they sat down to eat their meal, they looked up and saw a caravan of Ishmaelites coming from Gilead. Their camels were loaded with spices, balm and myrrh, and they were on their way to take them down to Egypt.

GENESIS 37:25 NIV

268   Fabrics and textures that make your skin tingle (in a good way). The sense of touch often isn't appreciated enough. It's good to give it a treat every once in a while.

269   The treasury of beautiful thoughts from around the world preserved, for our pleasure, in song and verse.

270   Thinking beautiful thoughts. Wherever you are. Just because you can.

Write about a song, or piece of music, that transports you to a particular place or time:

....

....

....

....

....

....

....

....

....

....

....

....

....

....

....

....

....

....

....

It is good to praise the LORD and make music to your name, O Most High, proclaiming your love in the morning and your faithfulness at night, to the music of the ten-stringed lyre and the melody of the harp.

PSALM 92:1–3 NIV

Find a book of great thoughts (or a book of quotes), pick an idea or two, and "discuss" them with the philosopher concerned. Write down what you discover:

271 Understanding that not every great thought has been "thunk"—so we should keep on thinking (and thunking).

272 Being able to talk freely about your beliefs.

273 Falling asleep unexpectedly and then realizing when you wake that (a) you must have needed that, or (b) you don't have enough cares to keep you awake.

....

....

....

....

....

....

....

....

....

....

....

....

....

....

....

....

....

Wisdom cries aloud in the street, in the markets she raises
her voice; at the head of the noisy streets she cries out;
at the entrance of the city gates she speaks.

PROVERBS 1:20–21 ESV

274 Going back to your childhood home. (Although you do have to sit down to be the correct height again to get the full impact.)

275 When what you want and what you need coincide.

276 Feeling happy just to be with someone (without actually doing anything).

Write about what you would (or did) look for on a visit to the place you lived as a child:

....
....
....
....
....
....
....
....
....
....
....
....
....
....
....
....
....
....
....
....
....

Even the sparrow finds a home, and the swallow a nest for herself, where she may lay her young, at your altars, O Lord of hosts, my King and my God.

PSALM 84:3 ESV

𝒲rite about a creative way you said thank you:

....

....

....

....

....

....

....

....

....

....

....

....

....

....

....

....

....

....

....

....

....

....

277 Falling in love. Sometimes it's what we want to do most of all. Then we discover we have no real control over the what, where, when, or who.

278 The things our parents and others did to take care of us so long ago that we have no recollection of them. If those who took care of you are still around, tell them thank you. If they ask what for, tell them you've forgotten but you know they deserve it all the same.

279 The maternal instinct. None of us really deserve it—but where would we be without it?

And while he was at Bethany in the house of Simon the leper, as he was reclining at table, a woman came with an alabaster flask of ointment of pure nard, very costly, and she broke the flask and poured it over his head.

MARK 14:3 ESV

280 The paternal instinct. Underrated and usually left in the background, but it is so often the solid foundation that the maternal instinct builds its "nursery" on.

281 The way a man and a woman are so curiously, fascinatingly, frustratingly different.

282 The way a man and a woman, although they are so different, can work so wonderfully well together.

Write down the things you most appreciate about your other half, how their strengths complement your weaknesses and vice versa:

....
....
....
....
....
....
....
....
....
....
....
....
....
....
....
....
....
....
....
....
....

Then the LORD God said, "It is not good that the man should be alone; I will make him a helper fit for him."

GENESIS 2:18 ESV

Write about your role in your neighborhood— what it is now and what you would like it to be:

....
....
....
....
....
....
....
....
....
....
....
....
....
....
....
....
....
....

283 Femininity, in all its wondrous, unpredictable, funny, crazy aspects.

284 Masculinity and its dependability (for good or bad).

285 Finding a space for yourself—either in your neighborhood, your work, or your peer group— where you can contribute something uniquely you.

Her neighbors and relatives heard that the Lord had shown her great mercy, and they shared her joy.
LUKE 1:58 NIV

286 The way children think you, as an adult, have read the rule book and know how everything ought to be done. There's a lot of security in that!

287 The older generation, who can teach a thing or two about how everything works.

288 Musical instruments, whether you know how to play them or not. It's nice to at least have the potential of beautiful music around.

Write down your favorite pearls of wisdom—and who shared them with you (older generation or younger):

....
....
....
....
....
....
....
....
....
....
....
....
....
....
....
....
....

For wisdom will enter your heart,
and knowledge will be pleasant to your soul.
PROVERBS 2:10 NIV

Write about a time you felt you were right—but felt being kind was more important:

....
....
....
....
....
....
....
....
....
....
....
....
....
....
....
....
....
....

289 Overcoming a fear, with the almost inevitable realization that it wasn't so bad after all.

290 Having someone meet you halfway because they couldn't wait for you to arrive.

291 Having someone meet you halfway in a dispute because they value friendship and happiness more than scoring points.

Be kind and compassionate to one another,
forgiving each other, just as in Christ God forgave you.
EPHESIANS 4:32 NIV

292 Public servants who, despite being employees, understand and value the service aspect of their work.

293 When the timing is perfect: when someone says the right thing at the right time, when the right person simply turns up, when you are in the right place to see something special.

294 That your life didn't turn out the way you planned. (Because you didn't know, when you were making those plans, half of what you understand and appreciate now.)

Write about an event or happening when the timing was out of your hands and out of this world:

....

....

....

....

....

....

....

....

....

....

....

....

....

....

....

....

....

....

....

When he inquired as to the time when his son got better, they said to him, "Yesterday, at one in the afternoon, the fever left him." Then the father realized that this was the exact time at which Jesus had said to him, "Your son will live." So he and his whole household believed.

JOHN 4:52–53 NIV

Write about a time you got to know someone's backstory and it surprised you:

....

....

....

....

....

....

....

....

....

....

....

....

....

....

....

....

....

....

....

295 That morning stretch where you fit back into your skin.

296 That there are people in this world who seem to exist solely to help others.

297 A friend or a loved one's hand wrapped around yours.

This is a faithful saying, and worthy of all acceptation, that Christ Jesus came into the world to save sinners; of whom I am chief.
1 TIMOTHY 1:15 KJV

298 Showing someone a little consideration (because you can and because we all need to be cut a little slack from time to time).

299 Being shown a little consideration. If you are in the habit of doing this for others, it will be a humbling experience, but you will understand more of what you are really doing all those other times.

300 That the situations and the lessons in the Bible are still being played out today—so we ought to be well prepared.

Write about a real-life situation that was nothing more than a Bible story updated:

....

....

....

....

....

....

....

....

....

....

....

....

....

....

....

....

....

....

....

....

....

All scripture is given by inspiration of God, and is profitable for doctrine, for reproof, for correction, for instruction in righteousness.

2 TIMOTHY 3:16 KJV

Write about a time a loss led to a gain or a defeat led to a win:

....

....

....

....

....

....

....

....

....

....

....

....

....

....

....

....

....

301 Giving someone something they don't deserve—even if you only do it to amaze them (but better if you do it to show them another way is possible).

302 Your defeats and what you learned from them.

303 Not always getting your own way—then coming to realize that it was better for you not to.

But whatever were gains to me I now consider loss for the sake of Christ. What is more, I consider everything a loss because of the surpassing worth of knowing Christ Jesus my Lord, for whose sake I have lost all things. I consider them garbage, that I may gain Christ.

PHILIPPIANS 3:7–8 NIV

304 Seeing understanding dawn in someone's expression.

305 That feeling as understanding dawns in your own mind.

306 The ability to make the best of things, however they turn out.

Understanding is a wonderful thing. Write about a time you helped a child understand something good:

....

....

....

....

....

....

....

....

....

....

....

....

....

....

....

....

....

....

....

The unfolding of your words gives light;
it gives understanding to the simple.
PSALM 119:130 NIV

Write about a currently good relationship that got off to a rocky start:

....

....

....

....

....

....

....

....

....

....

....

....

....

....

....

....

....

....

....

....

307 The fact that you don't actually burst with pride or happiness, even if there are times you feel you might.

308 Watching the rising sun gradually push back the frost line along with the shadows and realizing you can do the same with a frosty relationship.

309 Like-minded people (and belonging to a group of them who have good things in mind).

Barnabas wanted to take John, also called Mark, with them, but Paul did not think it wise to take him, because he had deserted them in Pamphylia and had not continued with them in the work.... [Paul said,] Only Luke is with me. Get Mark and bring him with you, because he is helpful to me in my ministry.

ACTS 15:37–38; 2 TIMOTHY 4:11 NIV

310 Keeping a secret to help or protect someone.

311 Being free of the need to keep secrets of your own.

312 The fact that someone trusts you.

Write about a childhood secret you were excited to keep (but only if it's okay to let the secret out now!):

....
....
....
....
....
....
....
....
....
....
....
....
....
....
....
....
....
....
....
....

Whoever goes about slandering reveals secrets,
but he who is trustworthy in spirit keeps a thing covered.
PROVERBS 11:13 ESV

Recall a place, other than your own home, where you had one of those deeply refreshing sleeps. What made it so?

....
....
....
....
....
....
....

313 Having someone you can trust. (With big things or small things. It makes no difference. Trust is trust.)

314 The good that a good night's sleep does for you.

315 The morning dew refreshing the world.

....
....
....
....
....
....
....
....
....
....

*When thou liest down, thou shalt not be afraid: yea,
thou shalt lie down, and thy sleep shall be sweet.*

PROVERBS 3:24 ASV

316 People who take the time, and have the passion, to become experts at wonderful things.

317 How little it takes, in the way of possessions, to live a truly happy life.

318 You might touch someone's heart for a moment with something you do or say, but the effects can last a lifetime.

Recall a time someone passed fleetingly through your life but left a positive impression:

....

....

....

....

....

....

....

....

....

....

....

....

....

....

....

....

....

....

....

When Jesus heard this, he was amazed and said to those following him, "Truly I tell you, I have not found anyone in Israel with such great faith."

MATTHEW 8:10 NIV

Write about something in your home (or something you would like to have in your home) that started off in a bygone era or originally had a different purpose:

....

....

....

....

....

....

319   Relics of a time gone by that find a new life in the modern era. A testament to endurance and integrity.

320   A warm bed on a cold night. Hot-water bottles. Electric blankets.

321   Waking up and realizing you still have half an hour to cozy in before the alarm goes off. That can be a beautiful thirty minutes.

....

....

....

....

....

....

....

....

....

....

....

*He will judge between the nations and will settle disputes
for many peoples. They will beat their swords into plowshares
and their spears into pruning hooks. Nation will not take up
sword against nation, nor will they train for war anymore.*

Isaiah 2:4 niv

322 Finding the first flowers of spring. It's like the moment you discover a promise is being kept.

323 Anticipation—the long wait you just know will be worth it. Sometimes it can be more fun than what you are waiting for!

324 Introducing an element you might not have control over into your life—like a puppy or a partner. An exercise in trust, hope, and faith.

Recall a time when you had to hand over control and wait, hoping it would turn out well:

....

....

....

....

....

....

....

....

....

....

....

....

....

....

....

....

....

....

....

I waited patiently for the LORD;
he inclined to me and heard my cry.
PSALM 40:1 ESV

Describe a face that fascinates you and tell why:

....
....
....
....
....
....
....
....

325 Things that have a precarious hold on life, reminders of transience and beauty.

326 Finding unexpected beauty in unconventional faces.

327 Finding beauty and contentment in aged faces.

....
....
....
....
....
....
....
....
....
....
....
....

"The Lord make his face shine on you and be gracious to you;
the Lord turn his face toward you and give you peace."
Numbers 6:25–26 NIV

328 Discovering your purpose in this life.

329 Seeing someone carrying a bouquet of flowers. Knowing that someone has been, or is about to be, appreciated is a real lift to anyone's day.

330 Being given a bouquet of flowers.

Complete the sentence "I am in this world to…":

....

....

....

....

....

....

....

....

....

....

....

....

....

....

....

....

....

....

....

*And in very deed for this cause have I raised thee
up, for to shew in thee my power; and that my
name may be declared throughout all the earth.*
EXODUS 9:16 KJV

Write about your favorite journey—or favorite way of traveling:

....

....

....

....

....

....

....

....

....

....

....

....

....

....

....

....

....

....

....

....

....

331 Someone offering you a supporting arm or a steadying hand (whether you need it or not).

332 Taking the slow train or going the long way—just because you can.

333 Rising to a challenge and taking the confidence gained from the experience into the next challenge.

The man gazed at her in silence to learn whether the Lord had prospered his journey or not.
GENESIS 24:21 ESV

334 Understanding that pretty much everyone you meet is making it up as they go along—just like you!

335 The right idea pops up at just the right time. How did it know it was needed? Where did it come from? It has to be a gift from above!

336 The rhythm of your heart. And the rhythm of the heart you first were aware of in the womb.

Write about your mother's dearest traits and which of them you see in yourself:

....

....

....

....

....

....

....

....

....

....

....

....

....

....

....

....

....

....

....

Adam named his wife Eve, because she would become the mother of all the living.
GENESIS 3:20 NIV

"*Joie de* vivre." *Joy of life.* Write about a time you were happy for no particular reason other than being alive:

....

....

....

....

....

....

....

....

....

....

....

....

....

....

....

....

....

....

337 The music inspired by the rhythm of the heart across the centuries and around the world.

338 Creating a new tradition among your family and friends—and hoping it spreads!

339 The sound of caroling bells. Nothing inspires exuberance and joie de vivre quite like them.

*"Shout aloud and sing for joy, people of Zion,
for great is the Holy One of Israel among you."*
ISAIAH 12:6 NIV

340 Singing with others. You are in tune in so many ways (even if not always in tune musically).

341 Writing or receiving love letters. Even reading love letters from generations gone by. Tangible proof of what matters.

342 Other people's bad examples—if we learn from them!

Write about a token of love that is precious to you, even if it once belonged to someone else:

....

....

....

....

....

....

....

....

....

....

....

....

....

....

....

....

....

....

....

....

May your unfailing love be with us, Lord,
even as we put our hope in you.
PSALM 33:22 NIV

Write about your dad's best traits and where you see them passed down in the next generation:

....
....
....
....
....
....
....
....
....
....
....
....
....
....
....
....
....
....
....
....

343 The fact that you are in a position to help someone. And understanding that we always are (although maybe not always in the way they expect or hope for).

344 Inherited physical traits. Free gifts from your parents!

345 When the bad weather gives you the perfect excuse to do those jobs around the house you have been neglecting.

As a father has compassion on his children,
so the Lord has compassion on those who fear him.
PSALM 103:13 NIV

346 A compliment from a stranger (with no ulterior motive) is like an affirmation from God.

347 The days when no one wants anything from you and you can please yourself.

348 When a worried child takes your hand for comfort and security.

What would you do today if you could do absolutely anything?

....
....
....
....
....
....
....
....
....
....
....
....
....
....
....
....
....
....
....
....
....

I can do all things through Christ which strengtheneth me.
PHILIPPIANS 4:13 KJV

Recall a wonderful gift—but write about the wrapping, the presentation, the hopes, everything that surrounded the gift without actually mentioning the gift:

....

....

....

....

....

....

....

....

....

....

....

....

....

....

....

....

349 The excitement of an unwrapped gift. A moment of absolute potential for happiness (made more nervously exciting by the slight possibility of disappointment).

350 Finding geometry and symmetry in nature. How does that happen (without a guiding hand)?

351 Sharing a moment of beauty that can't be expressed in words with someone who understands the importance of occasional silence.

But the fruit of the Spirit is love, joy, peace, longsuffering, gentleness, goodness, faith, meekness, temperance: against such there is no law.
GALATIANS 5:22–23 KJV

352 Despite the unimaginable number of people who have lived, there are still acts of kindness and love left to be done that are waiting just for you to do them.

353 The feel of the sun on your skin. It's like a caress from the Creator.

354 It is always possible to love someone, no matter how frustrating they may be—if only you will.

People can be trials. Write about the time, as a child, you most sorely tested parental love:

....

....

....

....

....

....

....

....

....

....

....

....

....

....

....

....

....

....

....

No discipline seems pleasant at the time, but painful. Later on, however, it produces a harvest of righteousness and peace for those who have been trained by it.
HEBREWS 12:11 NIV

Write about what the words *husband* and *wife* mean to you:

....

....

....

....

....

....

....

....

355 The words *my husband* and *my wife*. Full of excitement at the beginning of a marriage and (hopefully) full of comfort and contentment further on down the line.

356 If a bird or a butterfly, even once, feels you are a safe place to land.

357 A cool breeze on a warm day.

....

....

....

....

....

....

....

....

....

....

....

....

"So they are no longer two but one flesh. What therefore God has joined together, let not man separate."

MATTHEW 19:6 ESV

358 The opportunity to be extravagant every once in a while (without being wasteful).

359 The colors of nature that, somehow, touch your soul.

360 A moment to just sit and say thank you for everything—the bad for the lessons and redirection and the good because, well, good things can be taken for granted but they are always worth a thank-you.

Write about the colors of nature and what they inspire in you:

....

....

....

....

....

....

....

....

....

....

....

....

....

....

....

....

....

....

And the earth brought forth grass, herbs yielding seed after their kind, and trees bearing fruit, wherein is the seed thereof, after their kind: and God saw that it was good.

GENESIS 1:12 ASV

Write about a time you were someone's apprentice and what else you learned while they were teaching you how to do something:

....

....

....

....

....

....

....

....

361 Being or having a mentor.

362 Being or having a protégé.

363 Freshness—in flowers, in vegetables, in a day, in a person.

....

....

....

....

....

....

....

....

....

....

And he left the oxen and ran after Elijah and said, "Let me kiss my father and my mother, and then I will follow you." And he said to him, "Go back again, for what have I done to you?"

1 KINGS 19:20 ESV

364 Kisses—there is no reason why they should be so nice. But they are!

365 Laughter—it's an outlet for the heart.

366 The childlike faith in which a kiss makes everything better.

Write about your favorite kisses experienced or given at different stages of your life:

....

....

....

....

....

....

....

....

....

....

....

....

....

....

....

....

....

....

....

Let him kiss me with the kisses of his mouth:
for thy love is better than wine.
SONG OF SOLOMON 1:2 KJV

Write about a fresh start you made:

....

....

....

....

....

....

....

....

....

....

....

....

....

....

....

....

....

....

....

....

....

....

367 The fact that building a life or a relationship isn't such a big job. It can be done in a moment, providing it is always this moment.

368 The fact that living well and justly and beautifully, as Socrates pointed out, are the same thing.

369 Today is another opportunity to get it right.

Therefore, if anyone is in Christ, the new creation has come: The old has gone, the new is here!

2 CORINTHIANS 5:17 NIV

370 You know those people you especially love? You can love the whole world that way without ever having to reduce the love you give to them.

371 The choice between saying a negative thing and a positive thing is always yours to make.

372 That plants, apparently growing randomly and haphazardly, also contain medicines.

Write about a time you helped something (other than a child or a pet) to grow:

....

....

....

....

....

....

....

....

....

....

....

....

....

....

....

....

....

....

....

The righteous will flourish like a palm tree, they will grow like a cedar of Lebanon; planted in the house of the LORD, they will flourish in the courts of our God.

PSALM 92:12–13 NIV

Write about something you get to enjoy these days because of the generosity or kindness of someone long gone:

....

....

....

....

....

....

....

373 The people who just get you.

374 The people who don't get you at all—but still value you! (Those are special people.)

375 The people who planted the trees under which you sit on sunny days.

....

....

....

....

....

....

....

....

....

....

....

....

And Jehovah will make thee plenteous for good, in the fruit of thy body, and in the fruit of thy cattle, and in the fruit of thy ground, in the land which Jehovah sware unto thy fathers to give thee.

DEUTERONOMY 28:11 ASV

376 The people who umpire, referee, or adjudicate sports but never get to play. Including the soccer moms who make sure the teams turn up!

377 Flowers that bloom in winter. (And the people who remind you of them.)

378 Things that are ornate beyond all practical sense.

Write about something you keep in your life simply for its beauty:

....
....
....
....
....
....
....
....
....
....
....
....
....
....
....
....
....
....
....
....

He hath made every thing beautiful in his time: also he hath set the world in their heart, so that no man can find out the work that God maketh from the beginning to the end.

ECCLESIASTES 3:11 KJV

Write about your favorite creative activity:

....
....
....
....
....
....
....
....

379 Creative minds and the many ways we get to enjoy their outpourings.

380 Aching muscles. A sign that you have done plenty.

381 The fact that those aching muscles will ease and may have grown stronger in the process.

....
....
....
....
....
....
....
....
....
....
....

And thou shalt make an hanging for the door of the tent, of blue, and purple, and scarlet, and fine twined linen, wrought with needlework.

EXODUS 26:36 KJV

382 Finding a token of love that wasn't meant for you. Because, as well as having love in your life, it is good to be reminded sometimes that there is also love "out there."

383 Falling asleep on someone's shoulder...

384 ...and them not moving despite the pins and needles.

Write about the most romantic thing you ever saw that didn't involve anyone you know:

....
....
....
....
....
....
....
....
....
....
....
....
....
....
....
....
....
....

He brought me to the banqueting house,
and his banner over me was love.
SONG OF SOLOMON 2:4 KJV

Write about your favorite way to be fabulous:

....
....
....
....
....
....
....
....
....
....
....
....
....
....
....
....
....
....
....
....
....

385 Grass (except in mowing season). Left to grow long, it will make one of the most excitingly comfortable beds you'll ever lay down in.

386 The fact that life is always more vibrant and colorful on the side of the coral reef exposed to the ocean.

387 Having a "coral reef" in your life that you can shelter behind for a while when you are temporarily tired of being colorful and vibrant.

I am the rose of Sharon, and the lily of the valleys.
As the lily among thorns, so is my love among the daughters.
SONG OF SOLOMON 2:1–2 KJV

388 That you don't need to attend every argument you are invited to. You can also win by walking away (or rising above).

389 The fact that it will be all right in the end, and understanding that if it isn't all right, then it's not the end.

390 That you can stop worrying and the world will still turn and the sun and the stars will still shine.

Write about a time you defused a potentially ugly situation with a little imaginative diversion and distraction:

....

....

....

....

....

....

....

....

....

....

....

....

....

....

....

....

....

....

....

Blessed are the peacemakers:
for they shall be called the children of God.
MATTHEW 5:9 KJV

Write about a time when things shouldn't have worked out for the best—but they still did, and you got to point a finger heavenward and say, "I saw what You did there!":

....

....

....

....

....

....

....

....

....

....

....

....

....

....

....

....

....

....

....

391 Getting a glimpse into God's mysterious ways.

392 The smell of spring. It smells like...a promise!

393 The smell of winter. It smells like...clearing the decks for a new beginning!

But we speak God's wisdom in a mystery, even the wisdom that hath been hidden, which God foreordained before the worlds unto our glory.

1 CORINTHIANS 2:7 ASV

394 The smell of fall. It smells like...richness, fecundity, potential.

395 The person in your life who will listen to you talk lovey-dovey nonsense and think it sweet.

396 The person in your life who will tell you the short, sharp truth when you need to hear it.

Write about the place you most love to visit in the autumnal months:

....

....

....

....

....

....

....

....

....

....

....

....

....

....

....

....

....

....

....

....

In the midst of the street of it, and on either side of the river, was there the tree of life, which bare twelve manner of fruits, and yielded her fruit every month: and the leaves of the tree were for the healing of the nations.

REVELATION 22:2 KJV

Write about what your favorite outfit (for whatever occasion) does for you (in ways other than physical):

....

....

....

....

....

....

....

....

....

....

....

....

....

....

....

....

....

397 The person in your life who will keep secret the things you are genuinely better off not knowing.

398 Photographs of older people when they were in their prime—and the understanding that this is how they still are in their hearts.

399 The way high heels lift you more than just physically.

Stand firm then, with the belt of truth buckled around your waist, with the breastplate of righteousness in place, and with your feet fitted with the readiness that comes from the gospel of peace.
EPHESIANS 6:14–15 NIV

400 The words, people, or events that change the direction of your life for the better.

401 The fact that little drops of water, by patience and perseverance, can erode the hardest rock—and that love can do the same with the hardest heart.

402 The Japanese tradition of kintsuge where pottery is repaired with gold or silver seams making the vessel more beautiful for its breaks—and practicing it in our lives.

Write about something, or someone, that became better for having been broken and repaired:

....

....

....

....

....

....

....

....

....

....

....

....

....

....

....

....

....

....

....

For you know that it was not with perishable things such as silver or gold that you were redeemed from the empty way of life handed down to you from your ancestors, but with the precious blood of Christ, a lamb without blemish or defect.

1 PETER 1:18–19 NIV

Write about your favorite public place, exhibition, gallery, etc., and what it does for you:

....

....

....

....

....

....

....

....

....

....

....

....

....

....

....

....

....

....

....

403 Collections of art, books, fashions, etc., left to the public.

404 The ability to listen. Not only do you learn, but you also make the other person feel valued. Win-win!

405 All the creepy-crawlies that are so important in keeping the ecosystem working (as long as they stay in the ecosystem and not in your bedroom).

The whole earth is filled with awe at your wonders; where morning dawns, where evening fades, you call forth songs of joy.

PSALM 65:8 NIV

406 Home! Knowing there is somewhere you belong in this world.

407 Heaven! Knowing there is somewhere you belong in the next world.

408 Cotton. And the amazing people who figured out how to make that fluffy boll into crisp sheets and comfortable underwear.

What do you think is going to be the most wonderful, or surprising, thing about heaven?

....

....

....

....

....

....

....

....

....

....

....

....

....

....

....

....

....

....

....

There are also heavenly bodies and there are earthly bodies;
but the splendor of the heavenly bodies is one kind,
and the splendor of the earthly bodies is another.

1 CORINTHIANS 15:40 NIV

Write about the most exotic place you ever visited and the emotional "souvenir" you took away from it:

....

....

....

....

....

....

....

....

409 Suspending disbelief to give wonder a little more elbow room. Suspending self-reliance to give miracles a little more elbow room.

410 A handshake or a smile that just instantly connects you with someone.

411 Souvenirs from exotic places and your plans to increase the collection.

....

....

....

....

....

....

....

....

....

....

....

And she came to Jerusalem with a very great train, with camels that bare spices, and very much gold, and precious stones; and when she was come to Solomon, she communed with him of all that was in her heart.

1 KINGS 10:2 ASV

412 How making a decision turns a possibility into a reality. You just changed the world!

413 Being able to take (but not because you need to) an afternoon nap.

414 The gray days, physically and emotionally, that help us appreciate the sunny ones even more.

Write about the most enjoyable time-out you ever took, as a child or as an adult:

....

....

....

....

....

....

....

....

....

....

....

....

....

....

....

....

....

....

....

But Jesus often withdrew to lonely places and prayed.
LUKE 5:16 NIV

Write about the funniest sleepwalking, or sleep-talking, incident you ever saw or heard:

....

....

....

....

....

....

....

....

415 All the people in your life who have ever watched over you while you slept.

416 Watching over someone while they sleep, knowing you can't do everything for them but, for a few hours at least, you will keep them safe.

417 Living in the now, because the past can often be too heavy a weight to carry. Lay it down. Walk on!

....

....

....

....

....

....

....

....

....

....

....

*And they were all filled with the Holy Spirit, and began to
speak with other tongues, as the Spirit gave them utterance.*

ACTS 2:4 ASV

418 Electricity. How amazing is it to think that electrical and nuclear energy were there all along just waiting for us to discover them? What else might be waiting for us to wise up enough?

419 Wildflowers. A wild-flower meadow is one of the most beautiful things on this earth. Often it's a space man has cleared and God has filled.

420 Living a joyful life! People will tell you it is foolishness—but they will never have anything better to suggest. And you don't have to listen to them. (Which is often a blessing in itself.)

Write about the last time you were so joyful it crossed your mind that others might look askance—and you didn't care:

....

....

....

....

....

....

....

....

....

....

....

....

....

....

....

....

As the ark of the LORD came into the city of David, Michal the daughter of Saul looked out of the window and saw King David leaping and dancing before the LORD, and she despised him in her heart.

2 SAMUEL 6:16 ESV

Write about the ways people you know express their happiness:

....

....

....

....

....

....

....

....

....

....

....

....

....

....

....

....

....

....

....

....

421   Dogs with wagging tails and cats purring. Examples of pure pleasure.

422   Retaining some childlike delight. (You only need a little because it grows back with regular use.)

423   That scribbling down a note actually does free up space in your head.

Be glad in the LORD, and rejoice, ye righteous: and shout for joy, all ye that are upright in heart.
PSALM 32:11 KJV

424 That strength provides shelter for beauty to blossom and beauty provides a purpose for strength.

425 Heated car seats on a snowy day. (With a nod of appreciation to the many who have to walk.)

426 The strength to overcome a fear. (And the fact that it generally takes less than you thought.)

Write about a fear that turned out not to be so scary after all:

....

....

....

....

....

....

....

....

....

....

....

....

....

....

....

....

....

....

There is no fear in love. But perfect love drives out fear,
because fear has to do with punishment. The one
who fears is not made perfect in love.

1 JOHN 4:18 NIV

Write about the most ingenious way you or someone you know got your own way:

....

....

....

....

....

....

....

....

....

....

....

....

....

....

....

....

....

....

....

427 Someone coming from home to meet you—just so they can walk you home!

428 Confidence. (Knowing you will get it right because earlier in life you already got it wrong as many ways as are possible.)

429 Ingenuity. Anyone's. (But not a child's or a dog's when they are after something they shouldn't have.)

On Herod's birthday the daughter of Herodias danced for the guests and pleased Herod so much that he promised with an oath to give her whatever she asked.

MATTHEW 14:6–7 NIV

430 Waterproof skin, so we don't get soggy in the shower. (And the many wonders contained inside that delicate but strong and flexible covering.)

431 How the feeling you get from sharing is usually more valuable than what you give away.

432 Having a little gift of yours turn out to be really important for the person you give it to.

Write about a gift you gave that turned out to be more important than you ever could have expected:

....

....

....

....

....

....

....

....

....

....

....

....

....

....

....

....

....

*On coming to the house, they saw the child with his
mother Mary, and they bowed down and worshiped
him. Then they opened their treasures and presented
him with gifts of gold, frankincense and myrrh.*

MATTHEW 2:11 NIV

Write about an item of clothing that has an interesting story to tell:

....

....

....

....

....

....

....

....

....

....

....

....

....

....

....

....

....

....

....

433 Finding clothes, furnishings, or crockery that are so far out of fashion they are timeless—and cheap!

434 That elegance is eternal and independent of fashion.

435 Having clothes for every kind of weather situation.

And Rebekah took the goodly garments of Esau her elder son, which were with her in the house, and put them upon Jacob her younger son.

GENESIS 27:15 ASV

436 A one-off good deed that becomes a habit and then a tradition.

437 Learning patience—and having the insight not to be annoyed by the lessons that teach it.

438 The fact that the best answers and solutions are always beautiful.

Write about your version of "counting to ten." How do you keep your patience? And when has that method been most sorely tested?

....

....

....

....

....

....

....

....

....

....

....

....

....

....

....

....

....

....

A person's wisdom yields patience;
it is to one's glory to overlook an offense.
PROVERBS 19:11 NIV

Write a thank-you to someone who pointed out something you would be better off without, telling them how it has worked out for you:

....

....

....

....

....

....

....

....

....

....

....

....

....

....

....

....

....

....

439 Birdsong in the morning. It may be a functional thing for the birds, but it has an innate beauty that transcends function.

440 Setting yourself free from habits or needs that hold you back. (And the insight to recognize them.)

441 Kicking through fallen leaves when no one is looking.

Perfume and incense bring joy to the heart, and the pleasantness of a friend springs from their heartfelt advice.

PROVERBS 27:9 NIV

442 The desire to please someone. It's innate in all of us, but we direct it in different directions. Why do we have that desire if not to direct it up above?

443 Education. We grumble and groan at the time, insisting we would rather be doing other things. But nothing opens up the world for us quite like it.

444 A handwritten note in a time of texts and emails.

Write a note of thanks to a teacher who taught you, or to one you see doing a good job today. (Write it in the journal. Whether you copy it and send it is up to you):

....

....

....

....

....

....

....

....

....

....

....

....

....

....

....

....

....

....

....

Not only was the Teacher wise, but he also imparted knowledge to the people. He pondered and searched out and set in order many proverbs.

ECCLESIASTES 12:9 NIV

Do a George Bailey (from *It's a Wonderful Life*). Compile a tongue-in-cheek report of how awful the world would be if you weren't in it:

....

....

....

....

....

....

....

445 Discovering that even casual friendships can have unexpected depths. Those are the moments that turn casual friendships into something more wonderful.

446 Ice-skating on ponds and lakes, as proof that human ingenuity can turn almost any situation toward fun.

447 Being the most important person in the world for someone. (Or even just for your cat!)

....

....

....

....

....

....

....

....

....

....

....

"I have told you these things, so that in me you may have peace. In this world you will have trouble. But take heart! I have overcome the world."

JOHN 16:33 NIV

448 When someone takes care of something for you without being asked.

449 The rare and often beautiful things that are classed as "one of a kind."

450 Understanding that you and that one-of-a-kind object have a lot in common.

Write about the things *you* didn't get from inheritance and upbringing—the things that are uniquely you:

....

....

....

....

....

....

....

....

....

....

....

....

....

....

....

....

....

My dove, my perfect one, is the only one, the only one of her mother, pure to her who bore her. The young women saw her and called her blessed; the queens and concubines also, and they praised her.

SONG OF SOLOMON 6:9 ESV

Write about a fun, or uplifting, time that came from a supposedly solemn occasion:

....

....

....

....

....

....

....

451 Traditions with deep significance still being fun.

452 The phases of the moon. Just so we never take it for granted.

453 Whoever came up with the idea of cooking food—although mealtimes would be a lot simpler if they hadn't bothered.

....

....

....

....

....

....

....

....

....

....

....

....

So Sarah laughed to herself, saying "After I am worn out,
and my lord is old, shall I have pleasure?"

GENESIS 18:12 ESV

454 Being entranced by the gentle lapping of waves.

455 Your hair. It takes some looking after, but it is so worth it.

456 New experiences. Imagine how monotonous the world would be without them. (And if life is a little monotonous, we can always add a new experience into the mix to liven it up a little.)

Write about the last time you experienced something for the first time:

....

....

....

....

....

....

....

....

....

....

....

....

....

....

....

....

....

....

....

....

Then Saul built an altar to the LORD;
it was the first time he had done this.

1 SAMUEL 14:35 NIV

Compile a list of the things in your life that no amount of money could buy:

....
....
....
....
....
....
....
....
....
....
....
....
....
....
....
....
....
....
....
....

457 That you could have a new experience every day of a long life and you still wouldn't use them all up.

458 Not being overly attached to money.

459 The fact that we are in "the Goldilocks Zone" with regard to the sun. It's not too hot and not too cold. In fact, it's just right—for life!

But lay up for yourselves treasures in heaven, where neither moth nor rust doth consume, and where thieves do not break through nor steal.

MATTHEW 6:20 ASV

460 The ability to solve problems. (And if you don't have it, that's a problem that needs to be solved ASAP.)

461 Being serenaded. (If the singer has a good voice, that's a bonus, but it's mostly about having someone who is willing to embarrass themselves for you.)

462 A sense of self-worth—and extending the same respect to everyone you meet. (Because they might not know what they are worth until you show them.)

Write about a time you helped someone rise, even momentarily, from a situation where they had no hope:

....

....

....

....

....

....

....

....

....

....

....

....

....

....

....

....

....

....

Jesus straightened up and asked her, "Woman, where are they? Has no one condemned you?" "No one, sir," she said. "Then neither do I condemn you," Jesus declared. "Go now and leave your life of sin."

JOHN 8:10–11 NIV

Write about a way of life you would love to try:

....

....

....

....

....

....

....

....

....

....

....

....

....

....

....

....

....

....

....

463 That you can spin the whole world by doing a cartwheel. It's a foolish notion, but having a place in your heart for foolish notions is also a blessing.

464 The fact that circuses and traveling carnivals still exist and that people still want to live that kind of exotic life.

465 Stories that are so old no one knows who wrote them. But we still tell them and learn from them.

And the king loved Esther above all the women, and she obtained favor and kindness in his sight more than all the virgins; so that he set the royal crown upon her head, and made her queen instead of Vashti.

ESTHER 2:17 ASV

466 Poetry. The fact that it exists, the beauty it can convey, and the fact that we can all write it (to one degree or another!).

467 Just being outside, under the sky, after a day of being under a man-made roof. Some days (usually not the rainy, blustery ones) it can feel like coming home.

468 How the random combination of raindrops and a window (and the relative speed of the individual raindrops) makes a game that entrances children and adults.

Write a short poem about rain:

....

....

....

....

....

....

....

....

....

....

....

....

....

....

....

....

....

....

....

....

....

"Then I will give you your rains in their season, and the land shall yield its increase, and the trees of the field shall yield their fruit."

LEVITICUS **26:4** ESV

Write about the last really happy time you spent in the company of friends. (And while you are writing, be planning the next time):

....
....
....
....
....
....
....
....
....
....
....
....
....
....
....
....
....
....

469 First loves. How they rarely last and usually seem like no other since for the same reason. We really knew nothing about love at the time.

470 Spending an evening with friends, good food, and some silly games—and the feeling that the rest of the world may as well disappear because all you need is right there.

471 A moonbow. The fact that there is a moon to reflect the sun's light, the fact that there are clouds in the sky keeping the water circulating, and the fact that the clouds refract the light into rainbow colors are all miracles and wonders.

I am come into my garden, my sister, my bride: I have gathered my myrrh with my spice; I have eaten my honeycomb with my honey; I have drunk my wine with my milk. Eat, O friends; drink, yea, drink abundantly, O beloved.

SONG OF SOLOMON 5:1 ASV

472   A gentle mist that, rather than obscuring your vision, seems to soften the world.

473   Happy times from the past that have encouraged you through countless difficult times by reminding you that better is possible. You know; you've been there!

474   That in any gathering of strangers there is always the possibility of a best friend.

Write about a friendship (or friendly conversation) you struck up in an unlikely situation:

....

....

....

....

....

....

....

....

....

....

....

....

....

....

....

....

....

....

....

And they constrained him, saying, Abide with us; for it is toward evening, and the day is now far spent. And he went in to abide with them. And it came to pass, when he had sat down with them to meat, he took the bread and blessed; and breaking it he gave to them.

LUKE 24:29–30 ASV

Write about something beautiful that makes you cry:

....
....
....
....
....
....
....
....
....
....
....
....
....
....
....
....
....
....
....
....
....
....

475   People who have run the good race and kept the faith in ordinary life.

476   That as we get older we cry less because of pain and more because of kindness and beauty. There is no sense to it—unless kindness and true beauty are more important than people think.

477   Happy crying. There aren't many things more wonderful!

Those who go out weeping, carrying seed to sow,
will return with songs of joy, carrying sheaves with them.
PSALM 126:6 NIV

478 Trees that grow on apparently barren rock faces. Shrubs that grow in cracks in the architecture. If life can flourish there...

479 That ducks and swans that are usually not bosom companions will share the ever decreasing expanse of open water on a freezing lake. If only we would do likewise.

480 Radio waves and the fact that beautiful messages and important information (as well as nonsense and ads) can actually be sent through the air.

Write about a new technology that made a difference at some point in your life:

....

....

....

....

....

....

....

....

....

....

....

....

....

....

....

....

....

....

....

....

"See, I am doing a new thing! Now it springs up;
do you not perceive it? I am making a way in
the wilderness and streams in the wasteland."
Isaiah 43:19 NIV

Write about the last time (or the first time) you or your partner were foolishly, impulsively romantic:

....

....

....

....

....

....

....

....

....

....

....

....

....

....

....

....

....

....

....

481   Having a dream come true. Proof that you do, indeed, matter to the world!

482   Doing those little things people generally think of as menial as an offering of love.

483   Someone being foolishly romantic—a reminder that love is a wild, impulsive thing and more wonderful than many realize.

I am my beloved's, and my beloved is mine:
he feedeth among the lilies.
SONG OF SOLOMON 6:3 KJV

484 Watching a child absorbed in thought over something we would consider simple. Then imagining how our deepest thoughts must appear to God.

485 A loving touch for no particular reason.

486 That moment after a meal when no one wants to leave the table in case they deflate the love gathered around it.

Write about a family meal from your childhood, with honorable mention to the ones who were there but aren't now:

....
....
....
....
....
....
....
....

....
....
....
....
....
....
....
....
....
....

He offered a sacrifice there in the hill country
and invited his relatives to a meal. After they
had eaten, they spent the night there.

GENESIS 31:54 NIV

Write about the most fun you ever had in the snow:

....

....

....

....

....

....

....

....

....

....

....

....

....

....

....

....

....

....

....

....

487 Allowing the element of chance into your preparations—because you don't believe in chance.

488 Believing that the journey to any destination is almost as important as the arrival.

489 That fresh-fallen snow is like forgiveness, covering a myriad of imperfections and making all pure again.

Cleanse me with hyssop, and I will be clean;
wash me, and I will be whiter than snow.
PSALM 51:7 NIV

490 The fact that graffiti preserved across the centuries by being scratched into glass or stone is usually about love, hate not being worth the effort.

491 Adaptability. An essential survival tool in a changing world.

492 Knowing what you want and setting out to get it—while accepting that something better may derail those plans.

Write about the things you can do now that you were convinced you would never be able to do:

....

....

....

....

....

....

....

....

....

....

....

....

....

....

....

....

....

....

....

....

....

And Jesus looking upon them said to them, With men this
is impossible; but with God all things are possible.
MATTHEW 19:26 ASV

Write about a favorite smell and where it takes you to in your mind:

....

....

....

....

....

....

....

....

....

....

....

....

....

....

....

....

....

....

....

493 When you and your loved one say, "I love you," at the same time for no apparent reason.

494 The smell of woodsmoke on a fresh fall evening.

495 The smell of fresh-cut grass.

Pleasing is the fragrance of your perfumes; your name is like perfume poured out. No wonder the young women love you!
SONG OF SOLOMON 1:3 NIV

496 Seeing something you gave away in an unexpected place and knowing it's being put to good use.

497 Doing something for someone who used to do that very thing for you.

498 That even though theirs is a harsher world, even animals of the wild will sometimes do things just for the fun of it.

Write about something you own that you would love to know the history of. Maybe create a history that suits it:

....

....

....

....

....

....

....

....

....

....

....

....

....

....

....

....

....

....

For everything that was written in the past was written to teach us, so that through the endurance taught in the Scriptures and the encouragement they provide we might have hope.

ROMANS 15:4 NIV

Make a list of things you think humans might learn from animals:

....
....
....
....
....
....
....
....
....
....
....
....
....
....
....
....
....

499 That life goes on. And love travels with it.

500 That everything in the world has a purpose, a value, or a use. If only we could discover those assets before we make them extinct!

501 Horses. Power displayed in service.

The donkey said to Balaam, "Am I not your own donkey, which you have always ridden, to this day? Have I been in the habit of doing this to you?" "No," he said. Then the Lord opened Balaam's eyes, and he saw the angel of the Lord standing in the road with his sword drawn. So he bowed low and fell facedown.

Numbers 22:30–31 niv

502 When the enjoyment of planning a get-away-from-it-all break is almost as much fun as the trip itself.

503 The wonderful fact that you are not the same person you were a decade ago. And you will be different again in another ten years.

504 Music that made even the composers cry, like Handel's *Messiah*. Handel claimed he saw heaven while composing and could hardly see the notes he was writing for tears.

Write about songs that represent different times in your life:

....

....

....

....

....

....

....

....

....

....

....

....

....

....

....

....

....

....

For the creation waits in eager expectation
for the children of God to be revealed.
ROMANS 8:19 NIV

Where does your mind go when you are daydreaming?

....
....
....
....
....
....
....

505 Discovering that "home" and "family" might be different places and different people from what you might have expected.

506 That a perfect life is one lived in love. Neither is completely possible, but we can try, and our lives are improved by the effort.

507 Daydreaming. Where do our minds go then?

....
....
....
....
....
....
....
....
....
....
....

He said, "Listen to my words: 'When there is a prophet among you, I, the Lord, reveal myself to them in visions, I speak to them in dreams.' "

NUMBERS 12:6 NIV

508 Realizing you made a mistake or were wrong about something and having no problem admitting it.

509 Places laid aside in churches, public areas, or homes just for prayer (even if they do sometimes disguise themselves as other things).

510 The stars and the moon on a clear night. A reminder that beautiful things can come out of darkness.

Write about a beautiful thing that came out of a troubled time in your life:

....

....

....

....

....

....

....

....

....

....

....

....

....

....

....

....

....

....

....

....

Let not your heart be troubled: ye believe in God, believe also in me. In my Father's house are many mansions: if it were not so, I would have told you. I go to prepare a place for you.

JOHN 14:1–2 KJV

Write about the attributes you see in others that you would like to develop in yourself:

....

....

....

....

....

....

....

....

....

....

....

....

....

....

....

....

....

....

511 Having had enough prayers answered in visible ways that you can trust the less obvious solutions are also being worked out.

512 Peacocks shedding beautiful tail feathers and people finding and keeping them. The birds barely notice the feathers falling, just like people who leave beauty and kindness behind wherever they go.

513 Being brought breakfast, coffee, a newspaper, a flower... pretty much anything, while you are still in bed.

Finally, brethren, whatsoever things are true, whatsoever things are honest, whatsoever things are just, whatsoever things are pure, whatsoever things are lovely, whatsoever things are of good report; if there be any virtue, and if there be any praise, think on these things.

PHILIPPIANS 4:8 KJV

514 Pearls. Lovely to look at but also a reminder that irritations can have beautiful outcomes. (Pearls are formed around bits of grit that oysters suck up and can't spit out.)

515 Bad habits—you have kicked!

516 Someone seeing something good in you that you had no idea was there.

Write about the person who has believed in you most throughout your life:

....
....
....
....
....
....
....
....
....
....
....
....
....
....
....
....
....
....
....
....
....

From him the whole body, joined and held together by every supporting ligament, grows and builds itself up in love, as each part does its work.

EPHESIANS 4:16 NIV

Write about someone you could imagine as a living lighthouse:

....
....
....
....
....
....
....
....
....
....
....
....
....
....
....
....
....
....
....
....
....

517   Surprises. (But only the good ones!)

518   Lighthouses. They stand where there is the possibility of trouble and keep others out of it.

519   Halos on snow angels, because as well as having fun in the snow, something in us wants to be more holy.

Follow my example, as I follow the example of Christ.
1 Corinthians 11:1 NIV

520 Beautiful voices.

521 The number of people through the centuries who had to meet and fall in love to produce you.

522 Making a nest to curl up in when you don't feel well. Or having someone make it for you.

Write about your favorite way to recuperate:

....
....
....
....
....
....
....
....
....
....
....
....
....
....
....
....
....
....
....
....

*Immediately, something like scales fell from Saul's eyes,
and he could see again. He got up and was baptized,
and after taking some food, he regained his strength.*

ACTS 9:18–19 NIV

Write about the things you liked best about the family you grew up in:

....
....
....
....
....
....
....
....
....
....
....
....
....
....
....
....
....
....
....
....
....
....

523 Mothers. A good mother isn't a blessing. She is almost all blessings wrapped into one.

524 Fathers. If the only thing he ever does is allow a mother to be everything she might be for their children, then he will have done a lot. Some fathers do more!

525 Brothers and sisters. They generally go through what you go through growing up. Whether you always get along or not, they are proof positive that you are not alone in the world.

For whosoever shall do the will of my Father who is in heaven, he is my brother, and sister, and mother.
MATTHEW 12:50 ASV

526 The often surprising things that recharge your batteries.

527 Being asked for directions or help. It's best when you actually can help but, really, it's an honor simply to be asked.

528 Achieving something special by accident.

Write about what you think others see in you that would inspire them to ask *you* for help:

....

....

....

....

....

....

....

....

....

....

....

....

....

....

....

....

....

A new commandment I give unto you, That ye love one another; as I have loved you, that ye also love one another. By this shall all men know that ye are my disciples, if ye have love one to another.

JOHN 13:34–35 KJV

Not everyone raises their praise through the medium of song. Write about the ways you, personally, give your thanks to God:

....
....
....
....
....
....
....
....
....
....
....
....
....
....
....
....
....
....
....
....

529 Sharing a dream. Dreams are very personal things. Discovering someone has the same dream tells you a lot about that person's life. The fact that you feel you can talk about a dream with someone tells you something about them.

530 Hymns. And the fact that many of the hymns that have been sung around the world and across the centuries came from tragic events and personal experiences.

531 Knowing that your grandmother sang this hymn and loved it! (And hoping your grandchildren will feel the same.)

Rejoice always, pray continually, give thanks in all circumstances; for this is God's will for you in Christ Jesus.

1 THESSALONIANS 5:16–18 NIV

532 A deeper understanding—of anything. It seems there are always deeper levels, and the more science discovers, the less likely it is that all this came about by accident.

533 The childhood refuges, quiet places, and comforts you can still visit in your mind.

534 The way shared experiences create a bond not unlike that of family.

Write about the place, perhaps based on a real location, that you call up in your mind when you go in search of tranquility:

....

....

....

....

....

....

....

....

....

....

....

....

....

....

....

....

....

....

....

Now when Jesus heard it, he withdrew from thence in a boat, to a desert place apart: and when the multitudes heard thereof, they followed him on foot from the cities.

MATTHEW 14:13 ASV

Write about a time that patience and gentleness eventually brought about the desired result:

....

....

....

....

....

....

....

....

....

....

....

....

....

....

....

....

....

....

535 Green shoots that somehow push their way through the asphalt. How can you say anything is too difficult after seeing that?

536 Wise people (who aren't too proud to admit the mistakes they made that helped them get wise!).

537 Becoming wiser.

Be still before the LORD and wait patiently for him; do not fret when people succeed in their ways, when they carry out their wicked schemes.

PSALM 37:7 NIV

538 The fact that oranges come in bite-size segments. (And that so many seeds get wrapped in those delicious parcels we call fruit.)

539 When allowances are made for disappointments. It's an often unappreciated kindness.

540 When you taste the sun and the earth in a glass of wine and it becomes almost a cosmic experience. And why shouldn't it be?

Write about a time when you were disappointed and someone went out of their way to make you feel better:

....
....
....
....
....
....
....
....
....
....
....
....
....
....
....
....
....
....
....
....
....

"As a mother comforts her child, so will I comfort you;
and you will be comforted over Jerusalem."
ISAIAH 66:13 NIV

Compile a list of the things you appreciate about your other half:

....

....

....

....

....

....

....

....

....

....

....

....

....

....

....

....

....

....

541 When things are clean—even if only for a moment. It's a miniature fresh start.

542 When your loved one does something that leaves you thinking, *I chose well with you!*

543 The peace and security to fall asleep in unusual places.

Finally, all of you, be like-minded, be sympathetic, love one another, be compassionate and humble. Do not repay evil with evil or insult with insult. On the contrary, repay evil with blessing, because to this you were called so that you may inherit a blessing.

1 PETER 3:8–9 NIV

544 Inventions that leave you wondering, *How on earth did they come up with that?*

545 When you are having an on-the-ball day.

546 When someone else is having an on-the-ball day and you get to enjoy the benefits rippling out from them.

Write about the ingredients that make up a perfect day for you:

....

....

....

....

....

....

....

....

....

....

....

....

....

....

....

....

....

God made two great lights—the greater light to govern the day and the lesser light to govern the night. He also made the stars. God set them in the vault of the sky to give light on the earth, to govern the day and the night, and to separate light from darkness. And God saw that it was good.
GENESIS 1:16–18 NIV

Write about a time, recently, that you made someone's day:

....
....
....
....
....
....
....
....
....
....
....
....
....
....
....
....
....
....
....
....
....
....
....

547 The lyrics from songs of more carefree days that you will remember forever.

548 Providing carefree days for others.

549 The fact that oceans are ultimately made up of raindrops, which means that your efforts do matter.

Therefore we have been comforted: and in our comfort we joyed the more exceedingly for the joy of Titus, because his spirit hath been refreshed by you all.

2 CORINTHIANS 7:13 ASV

550 Memory; that we might have youth, friends, and family, even after they are gone.

551 Those horrible jobs we do when we are first starting out. They help us appreciate later, better jobs and remind us to be kinder to the younger generation doing that work.

552 That sanctuaries are places to visit—not to live in.

Write a note of belated appreciation to the stepping stones in your life—the experiences you had to go through to get somewhere better:

....

....

....

....

....

....

....

....

....

....

....

....

....

....

....

....

....

....

My brethren, count it all joy when ye fall into divers temptations; knowing this, that the trying of your faith worketh patience. But let patience have her perfect work, that ye may be perfect and entire, wanting nothing.

JAMES 1:2–4 KJV

What was the outcome that surprised you the most when you took a chance in faith and trust?

....
....
....
....
....
....
....
....
....
....
....
....
....
....
....
....
....
....
....

553 That we somehow remember the sound of our mothers' blood flowing around us when we are in the womb and turn it into the *shhhhh* sound that soothes and comforts our babies.

554 That beyond most leaps of faith are blessings we could not see from where we stood before we made that leap.

555 That absolutely everything in the world has a purpose and a place. Everything from microbes to mountains! How amazing is it that all of that fits together?

And Peter answered him, "Lord, if it is you, command me to come to you on the water." He said, "Come." So Peter got out of the boat and walked on the water and came to Jesus.

MATTHEW 14:28–29 ESV

556 People you only have a nodding acquaintance with, but you've known them so long they seem like friends—and they might well be!

557 Being happy with your own company. It's even better if you can be happy with your own company and still be a happy part of a crowd.

558 Always being there for your children but doing it in such a subtle way that they think they are quite independent. Like God does with us.

Write about a time you helped someone without them knowing they were being helped:

....
....
....
....
....
....
....
....
....
....
....
....
....
....
....
....
....
....

But when thou doest alms, let not thy left hand know what thy right hand doeth.

MATTHEW 6:3 ASV

Write about how other people see your home:

....

....

....

....

....

....

....

....

....

....

....

....

....

....

....

....

....

....

....

....

559 The knowledge in difficult times that there has to be something better. It wouldn't be so hardwired into us if it wasn't true.

560 Grandchildren! If you're a grandparent, you will know. If you're not— just wait!

561 People who feel they can visit anytime. It might be annoying. You might be busy. But it tells you that the world sees you as a welcoming soul.

"And if the house is worthy, let your peace come upon it,
but if it is not worthy, let your peace return to you."
MATTHEW 10:13 ESV

562 The satisfaction of a job well done (especially if it was difficult and you did it by yourself!).

563 Christmas. Regardless of how materialistic it is these days, it is still a celebration best expressed in love. And Christ is God. And God is love.

564 Hope. It's what remains when all else is gone. (Think of all the other things that might have been the last thing left in Pandora's box. They make hope seem like a pretty good deal!)

Write about a favorite childhood Christmas:

....

....

....

....

....

....

....

....

....

....

....

....

....

....

....

....

....

....

....

"Today in the town of David a Savior has been born to you; he is the Messiah, the Lord. This will be a sign to you: You will find a baby wrapped in cloths and lying in a manger."

LUKE 2:11–12 NIV

Write about the hopes your parents had for you—and consider them again from your adult point of view:

....

....

....

....

....

....

....

....

....

....

....

....

....

....

....

....

....

....

....

....

....

....

....

565 Seventy times seventy. It's the number of times we are supposed to forgive. Mathematically, the answer is 4,900. Spiritually, the answer is...always.

566 Getting an "I love you" from a sleeping child. Possibly the most honest declaration of love anyone could ever get!

567 Parents who walked a path you would like to follow. How nice to know they took care of many of the problems along the way before you ever got there.

Children are a heritage from the LORD, offspring a reward from him. Like arrows in the hands of a warrior are children born in one's youth.

PSALM 127:3–4 NIV

568 A home of your own, no matter how humble or how grand.

569 Having a purpose in life (and that purpose being to love!).

570 Struggles in life. Not for the struggles but for the person you are because of them.

Write a personal definition of "home":

....

....

....

....

....

....

....

....

....

....

....

....

....

....

....

....

....

....

....

....

A few days later, when Jesus again entered Capernaum, the people heard that he had come home.

MARK 2:1 NIV

Write about the weakness you are most proud of overcoming:

....

....

....

....

....

....

....

....

....

....

....

....

....

....

....

....

....

....

....

571 The Bible. A guide through this life to the next.

572 What the apostle Paul called the thorn in his side. That failing or weakness that encourages you to struggle to improve.

573 That one teacher, whether in school or elsewhere, who saw something special in you and helped it grow.

And lest I should be exalted above measure through the abundance of the revelations, there was given to me a thorn in the flesh, the messenger of Satan to buffet me, lest I should be exalted above measure.

2 CORINTHIANS 12:7 KJV

574 The thought that we probably have way more relatives in heaven than we have on earth.

575 Knowing you aren't perfect. What would be the point of a life where you didn't get any better?

576 Being busy—if you are busy in the service of good.

Compile a list of the things you do for others—then put your pen down and take a moment to appreciate how wonderful you are for doing all that:

....

....

....

....

....

....

....

....

....

....

....

....

....

....

....

....

....

....

....

I thank him that enabled me, even Christ Jesus our Lord,
for that he counted me faithful, appointing me to his service.
1 TIMOTHY 1:12 ASV

Write about someone or something you have learned to love more:

....

....

....

....

....

....

....

....

....

....

....

....

....

....

....

....

....

....

....

....

577   That every experience is a learning opportunity. Learning to see life like that is the first lesson.

578   The freedom to worship and to explore faith.

579   Love in action. Love kept in the heart is a fine thing, but shared with the world (or with family and friends) in lots of little ways, well, it's like exercises for love. It grows stronger with actual use.

Hereby perceive we the love of God, because he laid down his life for us: and we ought to lay down our lives for the brethren.
1 JOHN 3:16 KJV

580 People who go the extra mile when helping.

581 People who do good, even when there is nothing in it for them.

582 How a good laugh can redeem the most foolish of actions.

Write about an embarrassing moment that actually brought you closer to the person you shared it with:

....

....

....

....

....

....

....

....

....

....

....

....

....

....

....

....

....

The third time he said to him, "Simon son of John, do you love me?" Peter was hurt because Jesus asked him the third time, "Do you love me?" He said, "Lord, you know all things; you know that I love you." Jesus said, "Feed my sheep."

JOHN 21:17 NIV

Write about the time you wanted to run away but made a different decision:

....

....

....

....

....

....

....

....

....

....

....

....

....

....

....

....

....

....

....

583 Cheesecake. (And why not?)

584 The way good feelings create more good feelings. (Bad feelings create more bad feelings, but we are feeling too good here to go there!)

585 That the desperate thumping of a heart can inspire courage as well as fear.

A young man, wearing nothing but a linen garment, was following Jesus. When they seized him, he fled naked, leaving his garment behind.

MARK 14:51–52 NIV

586 Empathy. The times we just know, without knowing how, that someone needs a little extra love and consideration.

587 When someone understands, despite us having given no hints we are aware of, that we need a little extra love and consideration.

588 The tenacity to hold on when you reach the end of your rope, and the faith to know the effort will be worthwhile.

Write about a time you just knew (whatever):

....

....

....

....

....

....

....

....

....

....

....

....

....

....

....

....

....

....

....

For wisdom shall enter into thy heart,
and knowledge shall be pleasant unto thy soul.
PROVERBS 2:10 ASV

Write about the time a little encouragement from you made a lot of difference:

....

....

....

....

....

....

....

....

589 Understanding that there is something in everyone worth encouraging.

590 Emotional intelligence. Why is that a blessing? Don't ask for an explanation. It just is— and you know that already.

591 The times God communicates with us. When we can't put it down to conscience or intuition.

....

....

....

....

....

....

....

....

....

....

....

....

....

....

And when he wished to cross to Achaia, the brothers encouraged him and wrote to the disciples to welcome him. When he arrived, he greatly helped those who through grace had believed.

Acts 18:27 ESV

592 Being allowed (usually) to love whom we love.

593 Free will. Life would be so much simpler if we didn't have to choose between wrong and right, but having to make those choices and live with the consequences generally makes us better people. Almost as if it was planned that way!

594 The people who help us in ways we are unaware of. Like the mall guard who looked at his monitor, saw an elderly woman standing at an elevator after it had been switched off for the night— and turned it back on.

Write about how you met your true love (if you have):

....
....
....
....
....
....
....
....
....
....
....
....
....
....
....
....
....
....
....
....
....
....
....

Then the man said, "This at last is bone of my bones
and flesh of my flesh; she shall be called Woman,
because she was taken out of Man."

GENESIS 2:23 ESV

Write about something you were made to learn as a child that you really appreciate now:

....

....

....

....

....

....

....

....

....

....

....

....

....

....

....

....

....

....

....

595 The people who have helped us in ways we may have forgotten because we were children at the time, but they cared enough to make allowances for us.

596 Modern medicine.

597 Parents who encouraged you to do, or learn, things you didn't want to back then but are glad you did now.

After three days they found him in the temple, sitting among the teachers, listening to them and asking them questions. And all who heard him were amazed at his understanding and his answers.

LUKE 2:46–47 ESV

598 Finding the arms that will grow old around you as you grow old within them.

599 The way prisms split a beam of light into many colors. We need to learn to see people as being many-faceted and not just judge them on one "color."

600 That the earth's magnetic field not only protects us from harmful solar radiation but also guides the birds on their long migrations.

Write about someone you met who was more wonderful than they first seemed:

....

....

....

....

....

....

....

....

....

....

....

....

....

....

....

....

....

....

....

*Jesus saith unto them, Come and break your fast.
And none of the disciples durst inquire of him,
Who art thou? knowing that it was the Lord.*

JOHN 21:12 ASV

Write down as many childhood rhymes associated with games as you can remember:

....

....

....

....

....

....

....

....

....

....

....

....

....

....

....

....

....

....

....

....

....

601 Sacrifice. It's a strange but wonderful thing that doing without something for someone you love is really no sacrifice at all.

602 Having the courage to offer a helping hand. It looks easy, but what with fear of embarrassment and rejection, it's a very difficult thing to do. Kudos to you if you do it!

603 Proverbs, sayings, and skipping rhymes—how wisdom was passed down through the generations before Wikipedia.

He also spoke 3,000 proverbs, and his songs were 1,005. He spoke of trees, from the cedar that is in Lebanon to the hyssop that grows out of the wall. He spoke also of beasts, and of birds, and of reptiles, and of fish.

1 KINGS 4:32–33 ESV

604 Eye colors—and those that change with the mood of the person.

605 The fact that we have two eyes and two ears, so not only can we see and hear, but we also can judge where the sounds are coming from and how far away the thing we see is. Who came up with that?

606 Chocolate. (Well, no list of blessings would be complete without it!)

Compile an appreciative list of the things your body can do:

....

....

....

....

....

....

....

....

....

....

....

....

....

....

....

....

....

....

....

....

....

*"But even the hairs of your head are all numbered.
Fear not, therefore; you are of more value than many sparrows."*
MATTHEW 10:30–31 ESV

Write about a time you got to be a metaphorical bridge for two people separated by...whatever:

....

....

....

....

....

....

....

....

....

....

....

....

....

....

....

....

....

....

607 Starting off small—both in your life and your achievements. Because the only way to go from there is up!

608 Bridges. Very few of us will have physically built a bridge, but we use them most days without thinking of the time and effort they save us.

609 There's an old African saying "It takes a man and a woman to make a baby. It takes a village to raise a child." If you ever got to be part of anyone's "village," you were honored indeed.

And he arose and came to his father. But while he was still a long way off, his father saw him and felt compassion, and ran and embraced him and kissed him.

LUKE 15:20 ESV

610 That if you know enough people with enough skills, you can get just about anything done.

611 Having a skill that is particularly yours to add to the mix.

612 The neighbors you hardly know who would come running to help (although you don't know that yet) if catastrophe struck.

Write about the skill, or foodstuff, you usually contribute to a gathering. Recall how you learned to do that:

....

....

....

....

....

....

....

....

....

....

....

....

....

....

....

....

....

....

So he went and took them and brought them to his mother, and his mother prepared delicious food, such as his father loved.

GENESIS 27:14 ESV

Write about someone who appeared briefly in your life who might almost have been an angel for the difference they made:

....

....

....

....

....

....

....

....

613   That life has so many different ages and phases, it is difficult to be bored by it—if we're paying attention.

614   People who are actually spiritual signposts in our lives (and seem to be there for no other reason).

615   That, if we don't judge by the noise they make, we realize there are always more positive, helpful people around than the other kind.

....

....

....

....

....

....

....

....

....

....

....

Behold, I send an angel before thee, to keep thee by the way,
and to bring thee into the place which I have prepared.
EXODUS 23:20 ASV

616 Instructions. If it's not something you were meant to grow through by figuring it out, there will be instructions somewhere, maybe in the Bible, maybe in a foreign language—but somewhere!

617 The imperfections in your relationships which the Scottish writer Robert Louis Stevenson said, "continually spur each of us to do better, and to meet and love upon a higher ground."

618 Change. It may frustrate us at times, and may not always be for the better, but life is change.

Write about a change you encouraged someone in and how that worked out:

....
....
....
....
....
....
....
....
....
....
....
....
....
....
....
....
....
....
....

And Peter said to them, "Repent and be baptized every one of you in the name of Jesus Christ for the forgiveness of your sins, and you will receive the gift of the Holy Spirit."

ACTS 2:38 ESV

Write about some of the little things that make your day worthwhile:

....
....
....
....
....
....
....
....
....
....
....
....
....
....
....
....
....
....
....
....

619 The ordinary things in your "ordinary" life would seem like wonderful answers to prayer for many.

620 If you missed one, you might not miss it. If you missed a few more, you would be in trouble. Every breath you take. The breaths you take in your sleep. The breaths you take while apparently doing nothing. Breathing!

621 Small pleasures and how they sometimes go deeper than big excitements. (Not that big excitements aren't also blessings.)

For you, O Lord, have made me glad by your work;
at the works of your hands I sing for joy.
PSALM 92:4 ESV

622 The land might belong to individuals or companies—but the view is free for everyone.

623 Being asked—on any occasion, happy or sad—to be someone's substitute parent.

624 The many degrees of happiness, from a twinkle in one eye to jumping up and down, not caring who sees you.

Write about a time you took on an unexpected role for someone:

....

....

....

....

....

....

....

....

....

....

....

....

....

....

....

....

....

....

....

But after he had considered this, an angel of the Lord appeared to him in a dream and said, "Joseph son of David, do not be afraid to take Mary home as your wife, because what is conceived in her is from the Holy Spirit."

MATTHEW 1:20 NIV

Write about your emotions and their natural counterparts:

....
....
....
....
....
....
....
....
....
....
....
....
....
....
....
....
....
....
....
....
....
....

625 That the most powerful force in the world—love—wants to give you a franchise to work in its business.

626 Thunder and lightning—the weather letting off steam! And the fact that most of our emotions have their mirror in the weather, suggesting we might be intimately connected to a bigger creation.

627 Very clear night air, when space—and heaven— don't seem so far away. (Heaven isn't in space—but you get the point.)

Fools give full vent to their rage,
but the wise bring calm in the end.
PROVERBS 29:11 NIV

628   A neighbor you trust with your house keys and who trusts you with theirs.

629   Writing or sketching on a riverbank. There's a feeling that your mistakes sweep away with the current. If only we could transfer that feeling to other aspects of our lives.

630   The fact that the founder of the modern Olympics also instituted a medal specifically for fair play and sportsmanship.

Write about an example of fair play in ordinary life that really inspired you:

....
....
....
....
....
....
....
....
....
....
....
....
....
....
....
....
....
....
....
....
....

*For he guards the course of the just and protects
the way of his faithful ones. Then you will understand
what is right and just and fair—every good path.*

Proverbs 2:8–9 niv

Write about a time you asked for help and got more than you bargained for:

....
....
....
....
....
....
....
....
....
....
....
....
....
....
....
....
....
....
....
....
....
....
....

631 Surface tension is a blessing. The fact that water draws in on itself. Without it—no bubbles and, hence, no bubble baths.

632 Spa baths—and no one disturbing you while you enjoy one.

633 When you have to work up all your nerve to ask for help—and you get more than you could ever have hoped for.

Return unto thy rest, O my soul;
for the LORD hath dealt bountifully with thee.
PSALM 116:7 KJV

634 Play. Every once in a while it's nice to take a break from being grown-up.

635 Live music floating through the air from who knows where.

636 Rocking horses and rocking chairs, re-creating the rocking of the womb.

Write about an unexpected treat of some kind you got for free:

....
....
....
....
....
....
....
....
....
....
....
....
....
....
....
....
....
....
....

Now we have received, not the spirit of the world,
but the spirit which is of God; that we might know
the things that are freely given to us of God.

1 CORINTHIANS 2:12 KJV

Describe a design or style that really speaks to you:

....

....

....

....

....

....

....

....

....

....

....

....

....

....

....

....

....

....

....

....

....

....

....

637 Friends of friends. If you know nothing else about them, you know they have good taste in friends. The kind of person they are might also teach you something you didn't expect about your friend.

638 Design. Why is it that certain shapes, cuts, and combinations are just pleasing to the eye? (Also the people who know how to put those things together.)

639 Explaining sharing to a child.

And let them make me a sanctuary; that I may dwell among them. According to all that I shew thee, after the pattern of the tabernacle, and the pattern of all the instruments thereof, even so shall ye make it.

EXODUS 25:8–9 KJV

640 Homesickness. Why should it be that missing someplace is so much like a physical illness? Maybe we are all far from home and longing to be back.

641 Rain forests—so much life!

642 Having enough of a vocabulary to properly express yourself—but still having feelings that words could never explain.

Write about a time you spent adventuring in the wild:

....

....

....

....

....

....

....

....

....

....

....

....

....

....

....

....

....

....

....

And the angel of the LORD found her by a fountain of water in the wilderness, by the fountain in the way to Shur.
GENESIS 16:7 KJV

Write about one of those moments you wished would last forever:

....

....

....

....

....

....

....

....

....

....

....

....

....

....

....

....

....

....

643 That hard work is sometimes its own reward (which is just as well, really).

644 Poets that express feelings you didn't know you had until you hear them described.

645 Moments that you just don't want to disturb.

And the sun stood still, and the moon stayed, until the nation had avenged themselves of their enemies. Is not this written in the book of Jashar? And the sun stayed in the midst of heaven, and hasted not to go down about a whole day.

JOSHUA 10:13 ASV

646 Respite. When someone tells you just to leave it all and they will take care of it.

647 When someone makes something for you—no matter how skillfully or otherwise it is put together. They put something of themselves into the gift.

648 A meal that is exactly the right texture and exactly the right amount. You don't want to leave the table afterward in case you never find another meal like it.

Write about your favorite meal—ever:

....
....
....
....
....
....
....
....
....
....
....
....
....
....
....
....
....
....
....
....
....
....

And the king gave a great banquet, Esther's banquet, for all his nobles and officials. He proclaimed a holiday throughout the provinces and distributed gifts with royal liberality.

ESTHER 2:18 NIV

Write about the person (other than your significant other) you feel most in tune with:

....
....
....
....
....
....
....
....
....
....
....
....
....
....
....
....
....
....
....
....

649 Having someone stick beside you in the chaos of the city sidewalks.

650 Saving hard for something—then getting it on sale!

651 A friend who shares, and is your size, effectively doubles your wardrobe!

When the time came for her to give birth,
there were twin boys in her womb.
GENESIS 25:24 NIV

652 Baby things that get passed around, becoming part of more than one start in life.

653 Needing to buy something for someone. They get what you bought, but you get the pleasure of shopping.

654 Doing the laundry, or other household chore, as a gift of love for a family you feel blessed to have.

Write about something that has been passed around the family or down through the generations:

....

....

....

....

....

....

....

....

....

....

....

....

....

....

....

....

....

....

*Then shall the King say unto them on his right hand,
Come, ye blessed of my Father, inherit the kingdom
prepared for you from the foundation of the world.*

MATTHEW 25:34 ASV

What is the most inspiring story you know about from family history?

....
....
....
....
....
....
....
....
....
....
....
....
....
....
....
....
....
....
....

655 People who volunteer to work the holidays so people with families can be at home.

656 Being in the company of believers.

657 Grandparents or great-grandparents who worked hard to keep the family fed through really tough times.

Then Naomi took the child in her arms and cared for him. The women living there said, "Naomi has a son!" And they named him Obed. He was the father of Jesse, the father of David.

RUTH 4:16–17 NIV

658 Feeding ducks in a pond. Perhaps the simplest and most pleasant introduction to sharing there is.

659 Pretending to be brave—and having others believe it. (Although it's always nice to have one person who knows you better.)

660 That the money that seems to be paid out as soon as you earn it comes in just before you need to pay it out.

Write about your most unexpected windfall:

....
....
....
....
....
....
....
....
....
....
....
....
....
....
....
....
....
....
....
....
....
....
....

And because of the abundance of the milk they give, there will be curds to eat. All who remain in the land will eat curds and honey.

ISAIAH 7:22 NIV

Write about the best tip a grandparent ever gave you:

....

....

....

....

....

....

....

....

....

....

....

....

....

....

....

....

....

....

....

....

661   That Patty and Mildred Hill were inspired to write "Happy Birthday to You."

662   Surprise parties (you also don't have to clean up after).

663   Old recipes where half the fun is trying to figure out what the ingredients are.

Remember the days of old, consider the years of many generations: ask thy father, and he will shew thee; thy elders, and they will tell thee.
DEUTERONOMY 32:7 KJV

664 That all the effort put into becoming an accomplished musician or artist goes toward producing beauty.

665 That choirs enable weak voices to help in creating a beautiful noise.

666 Even the most stunning of diamonds needed to be cut and set for the best effect—so you can justifiably allow yourself a little extra time to get ready for a night out.

Write about the time your extra preparations really paid off:

....

....

....

....

....

....

....

....

....

....

....

....

....

....

....

....

....

....

....

On the first day of the Festival of Unleavened Bread,
the disciples came to Jesus and asked, "Where do you want
us to make preparations for you to eat the Passover?"
MATTHEW 26:17 NIV

Write about a time you were happier with what you got than you would have been with what you expected:

....
....
....
....
....
....
....

....
....
....
....
....
....
....
....
....
....
....

667 Organized get-togethers that are deliberately not organized.

668 Sea baptisms on a cold day. You know they mean it!

669 Fisherman's luck, which means being happy with whatever you "catch."

The grace of our Lord was poured out on me abundantly,
along with the faith and love that are in Christ Jesus.
1 TIMOTHY 1:14 NIV

670 Someone saying what they think (when you need them to) instead of saying what they think you want to hear.

671 A child's ability to bury "treasure" in the garden and be genuinely surprised when they dig it up again twenty minutes later.

672 Stealing someone's thunder. Maybe not such a nice thing to do—but an awesome expression. Imagine stealing thunder!

Write about something you laid aside and were delighted to find again:

....
....
....
....
....
....
....
....
....
....
....
....
....
....
....
....
....
....

Or what woman having ten pieces of silver, if she lose one piece, doth not light a lamp, and sweep the house, and seek diligently until she find it? And when she hath found it, she calleth together her friends and neighbors, saying, Rejoice with me, for I have found the piece which I had lost.

LUKE 15:8–9 ASV

Write about the time you were most out of your comfort zone for a good cause:

....

....

....

....

....

....

....

....

....

....

....

....

....

....

....

....

....

....

673 Feeling embarrassed volunteering at a soup kitchen. It gives you a little insight into how the diners feel.

674 People who have the knack of making those with no family feel like family.

675 That there are soup kitchens for those who need them.

But having suffered before and been shamefully treated, as ye know, at Philippi, we waxed bold in our God to speak unto you the gospel of God in much conflict.

1 THESSALONIANS 2:2 ASV

676 "As a man (or woman) thinketh, so he (or she) is." If we can train our thoughts, we can change our lives. And it's not cheating. It's a life skill.

677 Christmas markets!

678 With Skype, and other technologies, we can talk to loved ones around the world. With prayer we can go even further!

Write about a visit to a specific type of market and the most surprising thing you found there:

....

....

....

....

....

....

....

....

....

....

....

....

....

....

....

....

....

....

....

....

"In your marketplace they traded with you beautiful garments, blue fabric, embroidered work and multicolored rugs with cords twisted and tightly knotted."

EZEKIEL 27:24 NIV

Write about the aspect of your church that most appeals to you—or what would attract you to one:

....
....
....
....
....
....
....
....
....
....
....
....
....
....
....
....
....
....
....
....
....

679 The fact that churches aren't always full of "churchy" folk. Sometimes they are full of people who actually believe in the message Jesus brought.

680 That of all the attributes God could have claimed for His own (think of all those weird and crazy supposed gods from ancient times), ours claimed love!

681 They say you can't make something out of nothing, but you can double or triple a joy by sharing it.

Then the church throughout Judea, Galilee and Samaria enjoyed a time of peace and was strengthened. Living in the fear of the Lord and encouraged by the Holy Spirit, it increased in numbers.

ACTS 9:31 NIV

682 People who make the little they have seem like a treasure through their appreciation.

683 Sharing much-loved books with friends or children.

684 Visiting shut-ins and learning more about the outside world through it.

Write about someone who makes a little seem a lot:

....

....

....

....

....

....

....

....

....

....

....

....

....

....

....

....

....

....

When they had all had enough to eat, he said to his disciples, "Gather the pieces that are left over. Let nothing be wasted." So they gathered them and filled twelve baskets with the pieces of the five barley loaves left over by those who had eaten.

JOHN 6:12–13 NIV

Write a note of appreciation to the person in your life who has been the most help in the most ways:

....

....

....

....

....

....

....

....

....

....

....

....

....

....

....

....

....

....

685 Walking past the guy who has all the tools in favor of the man who has a heart to help.

686 When your family treasures are flesh and blood instead of porcelain and paint.

687 People who lift themselves out of a dark situation then go back in to be the light for someone else.

May the Lord grant that he will find mercy from the Lord on that day! You know very well in how many ways he helped me in Ephesus.

2 TIMOTHY 1:18 NIV

688 Putting love where there was no love.

689 That there is a big difference between value and price. Understanding and teaching that is a blessing.

690 Society makes a big deal about first kisses! But it was probably from a loving parent just after you were born. You have been loved and kissed for a long time.

Write about the most meaningful kisses (you can remember) in your life:

....

....

....

....

....

....

....

....

....

....

....

....

....

....

....

....

....

....

....

....

*Love and faithfulness meet together;
righteousness and peace kiss each other.*
PSALM 85:10 NIV

Write about a time your approach made a difference to a situation:

....

....

....

....

....

....

....

....

....

....

....

....

....

....

....

....

....

....

....

691   You can actually change your world by changing the way you look at it.

692   We were all helpless babies once. It's something every one of us has in common.

693   It's not the value of the gift that's important; it's the warmth it carries from one hand to another.

"The Spirit gives life; the flesh counts for nothing. The words I have spoken to you—they are full of the Spirit and life."

JOHN 6:63 NIV

694 The people who cheer others up don't always have better lives. They just try harder. We are blessed to have such people in our lives.

695 Offering someone who doesn't have contact with family a surrogate role in yours.

696 People watching. An insight into the truth about humanity—that they are mostly fascinating and wonderful.

Write about someone you know who tries harder to good effect:

....

....

....

....

....

....

....

....

....

....

....

....

....

....

....

....

....

....

....

*God did extraordinary miracles through Paul,
so that even handkerchiefs and aprons that had
touched him were taken to the sick, and their
illnesses were cured and the evil spirits left them.*

ACTS 19:11–12 NIV

Write about a time you brought two people together:

....
....
....
....
....
....
....
....
....
....
....
....
....
....
....
....
....
....
....
....
....

697 That someone without much who gives a little far outweighs a larger gift from someone who has plenty.

698 When enemies become friends.

699 That the best cure for loneliness is to cure someone else's loneliness.

Greet Priscilla and Aquila my helpers in Christ Jesus: who have for my life laid down their own necks: unto whom not only I give thanks, but also all the churches of the Gentiles.

Romans 16:3–4 KJV

700 Some troubles are like quicksand—difficult to get out of by yourself. But if someone standing on solid ground reaches out a hand...

701 That you can be "in a grind" or "in a groove." The smoothness of your journey will be entirely down to your attitude.

702 Sometimes it isn't what you do that makes the difference in someone's life. Sometimes it's just that you didn't stop trying.

Write about a time you were glad you hung in there:

....
....
....
....
....
....
....
....
....
....
....
....
....
....
....
....
....
....
....
....
....

*Praying always with all prayer and supplication
in the Spirit, and watching thereunto with all
perseverance and supplication for all saints.*
EPHESIANS 6:18 KJV

Write about a change for the better you made in your life:

....

....

....

....

....

....

....

....

....

....

....

....

....

....

....

....

....

....

....

703 Spotting someone at a fair, parade, or concert who would rather gaze at someone they loved than watch the main attraction.

704 A child's excitement at discovering something you already know, if it causes you to reevaluate your own excitement about the same thing.

705 The option to deliberately move your life onto a more beautiful or more meaningful course.

"In the same way, I tell you, there is rejoicing in the presence of the angels of God over one sinner who repents."

LUKE 15:10 NIV

706 Seeing your children become good parents.

707 Understanding that most of us have been blessed beyond all reasonable expectation—and giving thanks for it by helping others when we can.

708 That appearances can be deceiving.

Describe someone twice—showing how their heart is different from what their appearance might lead someone to expect:

....

....

....

....

....

....

....

....

....

....

....

....

....

....

....

....

....

....

....

All the people saw this and began to mutter, "He has gone to be the guest of a sinner." But Zacchaeus stood up and said to the Lord, "Look, Lord! Here and now I give half of my possessions to the poor, and if I have cheated anybody out of anything, I will pay back four times the amount."

LUKE 19:7–8 NIV

Tell the story behind a special piece of jewelry:

....

....

....

....

....

....

....

....

....

....

....

....

....

....

....

....

....

....

....

....

709   Paying a compliment to someone who is more used to complaints.

710   People who give less than they take and fix more than they break.

711   The groove a wedding band leaves on your finger. It is right that marriage and love should help "shape" you.

Blessed is the one who perseveres under trial because,
having stood the test, that person will receive the crown
of life that the Lord has promised to those who love him.
JAMES 1:12 NIV

712   That the age of your heart has nothing to do with the number of years you have been alive.

713   That if you actively try not complaining for any decent length of time, you will find afterward that there is less to complain about. Try it!

714   When fatherhood changes a man. (Most women prepare for motherhood all their lives; with guys it's more of a shock and wonderful to watch.)

Keep note of the positive and negative things you say in any one day. See which column is longest and take it from there:

....

....

....

....

....

....

....

....

....

....

....

....

....

....

....

....

....

....

....

....

If I speak with the tongues of men and of angels, but have not love,
I am become sounding brass, or a clanging cymbal.
1 Corinthians 13:1 asv

Write about a time you explored something new (for you) in the world of the arts:

....

....

....

....

....

....

....

....

....

....

....

....

....

....

....

....

....

....

....

....

....

715   Being awake in the middle of the night because someone needs you. With no other calls on your time, you truly are giving of yourself.

716   Hearing from a friend you lost contact with long ago. Appreciating the effort they went to to find you.

717   Ballet—from an era of longer attention spans and a greater appreciation of grace and elegance.

And thou shalt make a veil of blue, and purple, and scarlet,
and fine twined linen: with cherubim the work
of the skillful workman shall it be made.
EXODUS 26:31 ASV

718 Understanding that we are all, to some extent, like the Wizard of Oz—trying to be fabulous and hoping no one pulls the curtain back.

719 A favorite chair or a lap that you are always welcome on.

720 Understanding that you are not your emotions and reactions. There is a deeper, more real you under all the worldly stuff.

Write about a chair that had a particular place in the family or in your memory:

....

....

....

....

....

....

....

....

....

....

....

....

....

....

....

....

....

....

....

Since, then, you have been raised with Christ, set your hearts on things above, where Christ is, seated at the right hand of God.
COLOSSIANS 3:1 NIV

Write about a time when a fall in your circumstances enabled you to appreciate something you hadn't before:

....

....

....

....

....

....

....

....

....

....

....

....

....

....

....

721 Having all your senses flooded at once—which can only really happen in a busy city or the great outdoors.

722 How children who haven't met before can play for hours without asking any of the things adults find so important—like schools or religious or political affiliations or even names. They just need to know that the other child is nice and kind and fun to be with.

723 Sometimes when you "fall," you discover some surprising things. Like the child who tripped and was distracted from crying by the daisies in the grass and the colored stones on the ground.

Immediately what had been said about Nebuchadnezzar was fulfilled. He was driven away from people and ate grass like the ox. His body was drenched with the dew of heaven until his hair grew like the feathers of an eagle and his nails like the claws of a bird. At the end of that time, I, Nebuchadnezzar, raised my eyes toward heaven, and my sanity was restored. Then I praised the Most High; I honored and glorified him who lives forever.

DANIEL 4:33–34 NIV

724 That when it comes to counting your blessings there is always more than you thought (and possibly more than there are numbers to count them with).

725 When someone tries to steal your identity online but they get caught because they couldn't steal your personality, and sometimes that's better security than any password.

726 Discovering that people whose culture is worryingly different have the same hopes, dreams, ambitions, worries, and joys that you do.

Write about a time someone said, "That's just the sort of thing you would do!":

....

....

....

....

....

....

....

....

....

....

....

....

....

....

....

....

....

....

....

"Very truly I tell you, whoever believes in me will do the works I have been doing, and they will do even greater things than these, because I am going to the Father."

JOHN 14:12 NIV

Write about a sacrifice you made for love:

....
....
....
....
....
....
....
....
....
....
....
....
....
....
....
....
....
....
....
....
....

727   That how people treat you need have no bearing on the person you are. Shrug it off. Walk on. Until you find someone nicer.

728   When a child senses a sorrow or loneliness in someone and gives them a kiss or a cuddle or a comfort of some sort. They ignore the social protocols and the fear of embarrassment and do it just because it was needed.

729   When someone does something they would really rather not because someone they love needs them to.

Who his own self bare our sins in his own body on the tree, that we, being dead to sins, should live unto righteousness: by whose stripes ye were healed.

1 Peter 2:24 KJV

730 A grandfather who reckoned he had broken his finger, but when his two-year-old grandson tripped and reached out, grabbing that finger to steady himself, the man didn't cry out or draw back in case he scared the boy.

731 How everyone wants to be trusted with something and some people take the chance to let that happen.

732 That there are people in this world who won't let go of a situation until they can leave it, somehow, better than they found it.

Write about a risk you took in trust that paid off:

....

....

....

....

....

....

....

....

....

....

....

....

....

....

....

....

....

....

....

....

....

....

Now faith is confidence in what we hope for
and assurance about what we do not see.
HEBREWS 11:1 NIV

Take time to affirm yourself. Write a list of the things you like most about you:

....

....

....

....

....

....

....

....

....

....

....

....

....

....

....

....

....

....

....

....

....

733   Being the one who encourages your generation of the family to love and show love more. Just because such things weren't always so fashionable in tougher times doesn't mean they have to stay that way.

734   Taking every chance you can to remind the people you meet about something good they have to offer the world. Affirmation is a powerful tool.

735   Not letting only being able to do a little stop you from helping. Sometimes a little means a lot.

Yet to all who did receive him, to those who believed in his name, he gave the right to become children of God—children born not of natural descent, nor of human decision or a husband's will, but born of God.

JOHN 1:12–13 NIV

736 Looking on the bright side. Like when Charlie was hoping to photograph the sunset, but the weather was against him. "Still," he said, "the sun's not due to burn out for five billion years, so I might get another shot at it."

737 If you think of yourself as the only chance people have to hear something nice today and act appropriately, you will probably be right more often than you imagine.

738 When you can do nothing else, you can still encourage.

Write about the most encouraging words ever said to you or a time you encouraged someone else with surprising results:

....
....
....
....
....
....
....
....
....
....
....
....
....
....
....
....
....
....
....
....

So the men were sent off and went down to Antioch, where they gathered the church together and delivered the letter. The people read it and were glad for its encouraging message.

ACTS 15:30–31 NIV

Write about a time someone in a work situation went beyond what was expected of them:

....
....
....
....
....
....
....
....
....
....
....
....
....
....
....
....
....
....
....
....

739 Like the young mother who pushed her shopping cart and lifted things from the shelves with one hand because her other hand was cradling the head of her son who was sleeping in the cart, we often have no idea how much we are loved and helped.

740 The chance to properly appreciate a compliment giver (rather than politely brushing it off).

741 Colleagues who donate their paid-leave days to help you have extra time off work when you need it.

When Ruth came to her mother-in-law, Naomi asked, "How did it go, my daughter?" Then she told her everything Boaz had done for her and added, "He gave me these six measures of barley, saying, 'Don't go back to your mother-in-law empty-handed.' "
RUTH 3:16–17 NIV

742　The thing, or things, in your home working better than anywhere else.

743　Stepparents who take steps to be real parents.

744　The many and varied responses you get when you ask people to tell you something beautiful. If you're not seeing beauty at any particular moment, then ask around. It's always there.

Write about the effect a particular work of art has on you, whether painted or sculpted by a great master or a child you love. Or choose one of each:

....

....

....

....

....

....

....

....

....

....

....

....

....

....

....

....

....

....

"Your Majesty looked, and there before you stood a large statue—an enormous, dazzling statue, awesome in appearance. The head of the statue was made of pure gold, its chest and arms of silver, its belly and thighs of bronze, its legs of iron, its feet partly of iron and partly of baked clay."

DANIEL 2:31–33 NIV

Write about your wedding dress (or the one you hope to wear):

....

....

....

....

....

....

....

....

....

....

....

....

....

....

....

....

....

....

....

....

....

....

745 A wedding dress worn by more than one generation of brides.

746 The sort of people who don't leave anyone behind.

747 Being in a gallery full of priceless art treasures and thinking the most beautiful things there were the young couple lost in a kiss and the elderly man walking backward down the stairs so he could hold his wife's hand to make sure she didn't fall.

"Let us rejoice and be glad and give him glory!
For the wedding of the Lamb has come,
and his bride has made herself ready."
REVELATION 19:7 NIV

748 The opportunity to buy a "suspended coffee" or leave the price of a sandwich behind the counter so someone who couldn't otherwise afford it can have a hot drink or something to eat.

749 The way babies bring out the best in people. Apparently, tips go up in a restaurant if a baby is in attendance. When do we lose that ability?

750 The way our parents cherish the most unlikely objects because we made those objects for them when we were small.

Write about something your mom kept that you made or a favorite story she used to tell about you as a child:

....

....

....

....

....

....

....

....

....

....

....

....

....

....

....

....

....

....

*Wherefore I will not be negligent to put you always
in remembrance of these things, though ye know
them, and be established in the present truth.*

2 PETER 1:12 KJV

Write about the most creative or imaginative declaration of love you ever saw or received:

....

....

....

....

....

....

....

....

....

751 Unexpectedly having to ask your mom or dad for something, just like you used to as a kid. And they give it to you—just like they always did and always would if you needed it.

752 Seeing people who didn't have the best parents themselves buck the trend and become great parents.

753 The ingenious ways some people find to say "I love you" without using words. After all, love is also a verb, a doing word!

....

....

....

....

....

....

....

....

....

....

....

How fair is thy love, my sister, my bride! How much better is thy love than wine! And the fragrance of thine oils than all manner of spices!
SONG OF SOLOMON 4:10 ASV

754 That there is rarely a day that isn't the perfect day for something!

755 When someone charged with enforcing the rules decides to enforce kindness instead.

756 Planning and working in the fall so you can enjoy a beautiful spring.

Write about (naming no names) someone who bent the rules for the sake of a greater good:

....

....

....

....

....

....

....

....

....

....

....

....

....

....

....

....

....

....

....

And he said unto them, What man shall there be of you, that shall have one sheep, and if this fall into a pit on the sabbath day, will he not lay hold on it, and lift it out?

MATTHEW 12:11 ASV

Write about a community event you took part in and enjoyed:

....

....

....

....

....

....

....

....

....

757   Setting a good example despite being ridiculed by the crowd— because you know at least one face in the crowd is watching rather than mocking.

758   Remembering that those people who frustrate and annoy you are probably fighting battles you know nothing about.

759   That communal barn raisings and their modern, suburban equivalents still happen.

All the believers were one in heart and mind. No one claimed that any of their possessions was their own, but they shared everything they had. With great power the apostles continued to testify to the resurrection of the Lord Jesus.

ACTS 4:32–33 NIV

760 That we can be graceful in bad times—and grateful in good times.

761 You may not be the biggest fan of spiders, but a dew- or frost-covered spider's web surely will be among the prettiest and most intricate things you ever see. So, you see, they can't be all that bad!

762 We often whisper "Sweet dreams" to loved ones at bedtime, but it takes on a whole new meaning when you realize that a night in a warm, comfortable bed, wrapped in loving, protecting arms—a night you might think of as ordinary—would be a very sweet dream for many.

Write about a time someone showed true grace and the effect it had:

....
....
....
....
....
....
....
....
....
....
....
....
....
....
....
....
....
....
....
....

Then Ananias went to the house and entered it. Placing his hands on Saul, he said, "Brother Saul, the Lord—Jesus, who appeared to you on the road as you were coming here—has sent me so that you may see again and be filled with the Holy Spirit."

ACTS 9:17 NIV

Try to recall, and list, some prayers you are glad weren't answered the way you wanted them to be:

....

....

....

....

....

....

....

....

....

....

....

....

....

....

....

....

....

....

....

....

763 Finding ways to be thankful for the things that didn't happen.

764 The moments, often traumatic, that strip away the pretense and the cares of the world, leaving you focused on the things that really matter—love and life, health and happiness. The feeling rarely lasts, but it's good to have a reminder from time to time.

765 Giving someone a garden, either by letting them use it where it is or by transporting the shrubs and plants to them and then starting afresh in your own patch.

These all with one accord continued steadfastly in prayer, with the women, and Mary the mother of Jesus, and with his brethren.

ACTS 1:14 ASV

766 Finding the signatures of the builders somewhere around your house or a message left under wallpaper by previous owners. Homes benefit from a sense of history and continuity.

767 That we eventually become smart enough to make sense of the "nonsense" our parents used to say. (But by then we are usually too smart for our own children to understand us!)

768 The quiet servants of a church or a community who have been doing things so long and so well that most people forget they even need done and have no idea who does them.

Write about the parental advice that turned out not to be such nonsense after all:

....
....
....
....
....
....
....
....
....
....
....
....
....
....
....
....
....
....
....
....

Start children off on the way they should go,
and even when they are old they will not turn from it.
PROVERBS 22:6 NIV

Write about the thing in your home that the uninformed observer might think was most out of place:

....

....

....

....

....

....

....

....

....

....

....

....

....

....

....

....

....

....

....

769 Beginning things and not seeing them through is generally thought to be a bad thing, but the people who spend their own time and resources helping others make new beginnings without knowing how they will end are surely exceptions to the rule.

770 Thinking, "I don't have much in the way of possessions—but that means that when the sun shines, or a bird sings a new song in my garden, or a neighbor has a problem they need to talk out, why, I don't have much to distract me from giving it my full attention."

771 The church organist who was used to playing Handel, Bach, and Mozart but who didn't hesitate before playing "Twinkle Twinkle Little Star" because she knew how much it meant to the child who requested it.

The centurion replied, "Lord, I do not deserve to have you come under my roof. But just say the word, and my servant will be healed."

MATTHEW 8:8 NIV

772 People who still think to check on you long after the obvious period of grief and loss has passed.

773 The things that people are willing to do at no charge for people in need if they know about their situation. And the people who take it upon themselves to be the link between the needy and the people who can meet that need.

774 When your child brings a classmate home, not because they are a friend but because they need a little of what your home has to offer.

Write about the time you have been proudest of a member of your family:

....

....

....

....

....

....

....

....

....

....

....

....

....

....

....

....

....

....

Then Joseph said to his brothers, "Come close to me." When they had done so, he said, "I am your brother Joseph, the one you sold into Egypt! And now, do not be distressed and do not be angry with yourselves for selling me here, because it was to save lives that God sent me ahead of you."

GENESIS 45:4–5 NIV

Write about a time you stayed up long enough to watch the sun rise:

....
....
....
....
....
....
....
....
....
....
....
....
....
....
....
....
....
....
....
....
....
....

775   Getting up at 6:00 a.m. when you normally have to get up at 5:30.

776   Seeing the world through another person's eyes not only helps you grow closer to them, but it also helps you understand the world better.

777   Learning to tell the negative thoughts that invariably pop up in your mind to take a seat and you'll get to them later. Then forgetting to get back to them.

Very early on the first day of the week, just after sunrise,
they were on their way to the tomb and they asked each other,
"Who will roll the stone away from the entrance of the tomb?"

Mark 16:2–3 NIV

778 As a child, getting to the fallen apples before the horses did.

779 Feeding the birds in winter and getting to hear them sing in return. (A similar thing can happen when you care for a human in their personal winter. You are blessed for being a blessing.)

780 When someone is asked for help but thinks it might be a con—and they go ahead anyway because the slim chance they might be helping is more important to them than the larger chance that they are being taken for a ride.

Write about a place you weren't supposed to go as a child—and so it became the place you were most likely to be found:

....
....
....
....
....
....
....
....
....
....
....
....
....
....
....
....

When his parents saw him, they were astonished. His mother said to him, "Son, why have you treated us like this? Your father and I have been anxiously searching for you." "Why were you searching for me?" he asked. "Didn't you know I had to be in my Father's house?"

LUKE 2:48–49 NIV

Write about a time you, or someone you know, reacted to a worldly situation in a way that might have made Jesus smile:

....

....

....

....

....

....

....

....

....

....

....

....

....

....

....

....

....

781 People who walk the walk and don't just talk the talk.

782 The box where you keep your special things. (If you don't have one, you should get one. There are too many special things to leave lying unattended.)

783 Memories of time spent on a rope swing—and recalling the pleasure of flying without having to reexperience the rope burns and the sore rear end.

If anyone speaks, they should do so as one who speaks the very words of God. If anyone serves, they should do so with the strength God provides, so that in all things God may be praised through Jesus Christ. To him be the glory and the power for ever and ever. Amen.

1 PETER 4:11 NIV

784 A pastor who doesn't ignore the difficult stuff but still manages to bring out the love in the congregation.

785 Going to a busy person, rather than someone with time on their hands, to get something done. The busy person is busy for a reason. Likewise the person with time on their hands.

786 The people throughout history who have struggled to improve the lot of mankind.

Write about a historical figure you would most like to sit on the porch chatting with:

....

....

....

....

....

....

....

....

....

....

....

....

....

....

....

....

....

....

....

....

And [Jesus] was transfigured before them: and his face did shine as the sun, and his raiment was white as the light. And, behold, there appeared unto them Moses and Elias talking with him.

MATTHEW 17:2–3 KJV

Write about a cause you espoused or someone current whose work you think should be better known:

....
....
....
....
....
....
....
....
....
....
....
....
....
....
....
....
....
....
....
....
....
....

787   Having an outlet for beautiful thoughts, whether through articulation or art, music, or some other way. Beautiful thoughts are like sweet peas. The more you give them away, the more they grow.

788   Being a cheerleader for someone you think deserves more attention.

789   A book you read slower as you approach the last few pages because you don't want it to end.

I therefore, the prisoner in the Lord, beseech you to walk worthily of the calling wherewith ye were called.
EPHESIANS 4:1 ASV

790 Having luxury in your life—but rarely so you never get used to it and always get to appreciate it to the full.

791 Getting the chance to watch a wild animal do what it does, completely unaware that you are there.

792 Lighted makeup mirrors. They show every imperfection so you can deal with them. (If only there were similar mirrors for every other aspect of life and we were willing to make the blemishes they reveal better rather than covering them over.)

Write about an infrequent luxury you particularly enjoy:

....

....

....

....

....

....

....

....

....

....

....

....

....

....

....

....

....

....

He makes grass grow for the cattle, and plants for people to cultivate—bringing forth food from the earth: wine that gladdens human hearts, oil to make their faces shine, and bread that sustains their hearts.

PSALM 104:14–15 NIV

Write about an unusual definition of family that works:

....

....

....

....

....

....

....

....

....

....

....

....

....

....

....

....

....

....

....

....

793 Introducing standards and then, after a while, raising them.

794 The fact that an adopted daughter looks like her family, even though she isn't actually related to them. "Some families are just meant to be," her adoptive mom said. "You might have to go through a lot to find them, but when you do...it's just right!"

795 The fact that people can look very different, perhaps even be of different nationalities, and still be family.

For this reason I kneel before the Father, from whom every family in heaven and on earth derives its name.
EPHESIANS 3:14–15 NIV

796   Care packages from your parents when you are far from home.

797   Being able to send care packages to people and places you don't know and might never visit. But your love will visit, and the people will know you by that.

798   How our interpretation of important work changes as we travel through life.

Write about the most fulfilling work you do:

....

....

....

....

....

....

....

....

....

....

....

....

....

....

....

....

....

....

....

Therefore, my dear friends, as you have always obeyed—not only in my presence, but now much more in my absence—continue to work out your salvation with fear and trembling, for it is God who works in you to will and to act in order to fulfill his good purpose.

PHILIPPIANS 2:12–13 NIV

Write about a friend from a different generation and how the friendship came about:

....
....
....
....
....
....
....
....
....
....
....
....
....
....
....
....
....

799 Smiling at someone who never returns it—until they do!

800 Being generous with our money, as a stepping-stone toward being generous with ourselves.

801 Becoming friends with someone despite a huge disparity between your ages—and discovering that apart from adding a new depth to the shared experiences, the age thing makes no difference.

After spending some time there, they were sent off by the believers with the blessing of peace to return to those who had sent them.

ACTS 15:33 NIV

802 When a new neighbor wants to talk to you about the noise your children make. And he tells you it lifts his spirits hearing them have fun.

803 Cathedrals. Not because they necessarily bring anyone closer to God, but because in seeking to praise Him, mankind can often rise to some impressive heights.

804 Your immune system. It's like you have an army of miniature doctors running around inside you saving you from "bad guys" too small for you to see.

Write a thank-you to someone who cared for you one time you were ill:

....

....

....

....

....

....

....

....

....

....

....

....

....

....

....

....

....

....

When he heard this, Jesus said, "This sickness will not end in death. No, it is for God's glory so that God's Son may be glorified through it."

JOHN 11:4 NIV

Write about the regular chores you and your siblings did as children:

....

....

....

....

....

....

....

....

....

....

....

....

....

....

....

....

....

....

805 Indoor plumbing. Not only is it more sanitary and helps prevent disease, but it also does away with those cold, after-dark visits to the outhouse.

806 The bond that comes from sharing boring chores with someone.

807 Someone who will stand by you when no one else will, because we all mess up once in a while. (And being that person for someone else.)

In addition, they distributed to the males three years old or more whose names were in the genealogical records—all who would enter the temple of the LORD to perform the daily duties of their various tasks, according to their responsibilities and their divisions.

2 CHRONICLES 31:16 NIV

808 A buttercup will try to outgrow roses in its quest for the sun because it isn't concerned with the ability of the rose; it is solely focused on the sun. Take a lesson from the buttercup when it comes to matters of faith.

809 That being a little cog in a great big machine is nothing to be looked down upon. You know what happens to great big machines when you take even a little cog away.

810 Faking needing to be helped so someone else will forget they might have needed help, because they are too busy "helping" you.

Write about a small but essential part you played in some recent venture:

....

....

....

....

....

....

....

....

....

....

....

....

....

....

....

....

....

....

....

....

As the soldiers led him away, they seized Simon from Cyrene, who was on his way in from the country, and put the cross on him and made him carry it behind Jesus.

LUKE 23:26 NIV

Write about a time someone set you a challenge—and you met it:

....

....

....

....

....

....

....

....

....

....

....

....

....

....

....

....

....

....

811   When someone put a note on a prayer tree requesting "that my friend be happy again" and the next day an anonymous someone thumbtacked a cinema gift card to the tree with a note saying "For your friend."

812   That if you expect great things of people, they will generally try their best not to disappoint you. (And they may surprise themselves.)

813   When you do a little kindness and the recipient says, "That's the nicest thing anyone has ever done for me," and you realize they aren't just being polite; they really mean it. That's a time to reassess all your own blessings.

But since you excel in everything—in faith, in speech, in knowledge, in complete earnestness and in the love we have kindled in you— see that you also excel in this grace of giving.

2 CORINTHIANS 8:7 NIV

814 When a new baby receives a gift from a friend of a friend of a friend (whom they might never meet) just for being born.

815 When a child wants to be just like you—and you reassess what being "you" means. Then maybe both of you can be like the best of you.

816 Personal victories and the people who make others feel it's okay to come back. Like when the woman Sue was talking to stood up in the middle of their conversation and left—only to return five minutes later. "Sometimes I can't handle people and I run away," she explained. "But this time I came back."

Write about a time you unwittingly found yourself being a role model for someone:

....

....

....

....

....

....

....

....

....

....

....

....

....

....

....

....

....

....

I commend to you our sister Phoebe, a deacon of the church in Cenchreae. I ask you to receive her in the Lord in a way worthy of his people and to give her any help she may need from you, for she has been the benefactor of many people, including me.

ROMANS 16:1–2 NIV

Write about someone you met who seemed to infuse an uninspiring job with an uplifting attitude:

....
....
....
....
....
....
....
....
....
....
....
....
....
....
....
....
....
....
....
....
....

817 The people whose love for you has helped you learn how to love yourself better.

818 Farmers markets.

819 That we can all brighten our work space, whether it's at home, in an office, or out and about. If we can't take flowers and framed photos with us, we can take our smile, a sunnier attitude, a plentiful supply of friendly words, or even just kinder thoughts.

I know that when I come to you, I will come in the full measure of the blessing of Christ.
ROMANS 15:29 NIV

820   That the best way to get even with someone who does you a bad turn is to get better and live the kind of life their negativity tried to stifle.

821   The delight children take in stones from the ground is a reminder that everything has value and beauty if we can only learn to see it how its Creator (and children) see it.

822   That a broken friendship if properly mended, like a broken bone properly healed, can be stronger because of the trauma that tried to break it. Life can have all sorts of "breaks"; the challenge is to find the proper "healing."

Write about a relationship you healed or helped heal:

....

....

....

....

....

....

....

....

....

....

....

....

....

....

....

....

....

....

....

....

*Make every effort to keep the unity of
the Spirit through the bond of peace.*
EPHESIANS 4:3 NIV

Write about a time you glimpsed the real man or woman behind the stereotype of a homeless person or an addict:

....

....

....

....

....

....

....

....

....

....

....

....

....

....

....

....

....

....

....

....

....

823 That there are people in the world who will still try to help those who are surely lost causes...

824 ...and that they often succeed, proving there is no such thing as a lost cause in this world...

825 ...and that they were also considered lost causes at one time or another.

Then Judas, who betrayed him, when he saw that he was condemned, repented himself, and brought back the thirty pieces of silver to the chief priests and elders.

MATTHEW 27:3 ASV

826 Greetings for strangers that involve kisses, hugs, and garlands of flowers—if only we could move beyond the ceremony, look past the embarrassment, and get back to the original intent and heart of the greeting.

827 That the seasons of the year so accurately reflect the seasons of your life. Always remembering that after the winter comes another spring.

828 Faithfulness, whether between a pet and its owner, a spouse and their partner, a person and God, or a person and their principles. It is the attribute that so much good gets built upon.

Write about a favorite pet (either yours or a friend's) and its loyalty:

....

....

....

....

....

....

....

....

....

....

....

....

....

....

....

....

....

....

"Lord, the God of our fathers Abraham, Isaac and Israel, keep these desires and thoughts in the hearts of your people forever, and keep their hearts loyal to you."
1 Chronicles 29:18 niv

Write about a time you got to be a voice of wisdom for a friend:

....
....
....
....
....
....
....
....
....
....
....
....
....
....
....
....
....
....
....
....

829 The quiet voice in your head that generally knows the right thing to do—but never forces you to listen. How like God does that sound?

830 Listening for that voice more and more. Coming to expect it, getting used to doing what it says until it becomes your primary thought—even if it doesn't originate from you.

831 Remembering that there are other voices in there clamoring for attention, but they aren't your friends, and you can tell that by the messages of fear and doubt they peddle.

"Think how you have instructed many, how you have strengthened feeble hands. Your words have supported those who stumbled; you have strengthened faltering knees."

JOB 4:3–4 NIV

832 Language teachers in the Far East sometimes advertise courses in Important English. They teach words and phrases based on how useful they will be to the pupil. Words do have power. We might take time to make sure the language we use is "important."

833 That diamonds are just dull lumps of buried coal—before pressure is applied. Are you thankful for the pressure in your life?

834 Getting something for free—and passing it on as a gift. You are not being cheap; you are doubling the bounty and spreading the joy!

Compile a list of words and phrases you would teach as "important" English. Make sure they reflect your priorities while still being useful:

....

....

....

....

....

....

....

....

....

....

....

....

....

....

....

....

....

....

All your words are true; all your righteous laws are eternal.
PSALM 119:160 NIV

Write about a time you tried to get closer to something wonderful:

....
....
....
....
....
....
....
....
....
....
....
....
....
....
....
....
....
....
....
....

835 Weddings. When two become one in a reflection of the perfect relationship between mankind and God. Unless, that is, one of the two puts themselves first, ahead of the union.

836 The rocks in a stream cause the water to froth and tumble, cleaning the stream and (some romantics suggest) making it sing. What are the "rocks" in your "stream" doing for you?

837 That rainbows move away as you approach them. Some dreams, like heaven and rainbows, are for pursuing, not catching. In this life, anyway!

When Moses came down from Mount Sinai with the two tablets of the covenant law in his hands, he was not aware that his face was radiant because he had spoken with the Lord.

Exodus 34:29 NIV

838 When the weather (whatever kind it is) is so intense you just have to put everything else aside and enjoy it.

839 People who are serious about their work—but can't hide the fact that they love it!

840 The place you are un-likely to be disturbed—like the fire escape (unless you are disturbed by others looking for a place where they wouldn't be disturbed).

Write about your favorite kind of weather and a time it really showed itself off:

....

....

....

....

....

....

....

....

....

....

....

....

....

....

....

....

....

And he saith unto them, Why are ye fearful, O ye of little faith? Then he arose, and rebuked the winds and the sea; and there was a great calm. And the men marvelled, saying, What manner of man is this, that even the winds and the sea obey him?

MATTHEW 8:26–27 ASV

Write about the time you discovered, or uncovered, the person behind the mask someone presented to the world:

....

....

....

....

....

....

....

....

....

....

....

....

....

....

....

....

....

....

....

841 Masked balls, encouraging thoughts of who or what you might be if no one knew who you were. And the realization that all of that is still possible once you lay aside the mask you wear on a daily basis.

842 Butterflies in your stomach when The One walks into the room— even if you have been married for decades! It's hard to imagine a good biological explanation for the phenomenon, but it is a delight!

843 The ones who take the risks and make the discoveries the rest of us homebodies come to appreciate and depend on.

That which is born of the flesh is flesh; and that which is born of the Spirit is spirit. Marvel not that I said unto thee, Ye must be born anew.
JOHN 3:6–7 ASV

844 People who hold an elevator door open for you. There's really nothing in it for them. You decrease their available space, and you might be really obnoxious. But they are prepared to take that chance for you.

845 The friend who brought you and your other half together. (Sure, they might also be responsible for a few bad times, but when it's all shaken down, you owe them big-time!)

846 Airshows—and the little bird that decides to entertain the audience by showing what it can do.

Write a thank-you to the person, or situation, that brought you and your partner together. (Or a note listing your "requirements" if it hasn't happened yet):

....

....

....

....

....

....

....

....

....

....

....

....

....

....

....

....

....

....

Jehovah grant you that ye may find rest, each of you in the house of her husband. Then she kissed them, and they lifted up their voice, and wept.

RUTH 1:9 ASV

Write about the way faith, or love, has made a difference in your life:

....

....

....

....

....

....

....

....

....

....

....

....

....

....

....

....

....

....

....

....

847 You get down close and inspect something that grew in the dirt and you remember the same stuff also provided the material for the first man. Dirt is way more wonderful than it seems.

848 If this world was as some would have it—a random accident or an arena in which only the fittest of genes survive— then there would be no place for beauty, kindness, or altruism. But those qualities exist in abundance!

849 That the more you give thanks, the more you find to give thanks for. Coincidence?

"By faith in the name of Jesus, this man whom you see and know was made strong. It is Jesus' name and the faith that comes through him that has completely healed him, as you can all see."

ACTS 3:16 NIV

850 People who add a touch of style to monotonous jobs—like the guard on the early train who asked all the passengers to have their tickets and smiles available for inspection.

851 When you find someone with a self-destructive habit and you talk to them as a person of more worth than they seem to be giving themselves.

852 The opportunity to give more than was expected to someone who had a difficult time asking for help.

Write about someone in an uninspiring situation who added (or adds) a little extra:

....

....

....

....

....

....

....

....

....

....

....

....

....

....

....

....

....

"Suppose one of you has a hundred sheep and loses one of them. Doesn't he leave the ninety-nine in the open country and go after the lost sheep until he finds it? And when he finds it, he joyfully puts it on his shoulders."

LUKE 15:4–5 NIV

Write about something in nature that recently took your breath away:

....

....

....

....

....

....

....

....

....

....

....

....

....

....

....

....

....

....

....

853 When a home move falls through and you are disappointed—but the friends and neighbors who were so supportive of your decision to move throw a party because you're staying.

854 Girl stuff and boy stuff that gets faithfully passed down through the female and male strands of the many generations just because it's really useful or really interesting—or fun.

855 Meteor showers. Something to watch in company in the fresh night air and be amazed by.

And Moses stretched out his hand over the sea; and the LORD caused the sea to go back by a strong east wind all that night, and made the sea dry land, and the waters were divided.

EXODUS 14:21 KJV

856 When strong independent men allow you to help them with something you might just possibly be (slightly) better at.

857 The owner of a diner who took customer care to a new level when she delivered lunches to a customer who never really talked to her but who was in the hospital. She knew he wouldn't eat if things weren't arranged "just so," and she knew how to do that.

858 When you see the lessons you tried so hard to impart to your children—which they seemed to try really hard to ignore—blossoming in their children and you realize they were listening after all.

Write about a time when weakness was actually a strength:

....

....

....

....

....

....

....

....

....

....

....

....

....

....

....

....

....

....

....

....

....

God chose the lowly things of this world and the despised things—and the things that are not—to nullify the things that are.

1 CORINTHIANS 1:28 NIV

Write about the place you go (outside of church, perhaps) just to reconnect with your soul:

....
....
....
....
....
....
....
....
....
....
....
....
....
....
....
....
....
....
....

859 Having a place in your life, like a favorite museum, that seems to provide stability and continuity and always makes you feel welcome no matter how long it has been since your last visit.

860 Water flowing from an overflow pipe on the side of an ugly old building is lifted into a spray in the crisp evening air, and the setting sun refracts in the scattered drops creating an impromptu rainbow. Beauty can appear at any time and in the most unexpected circumstances.

861 Grace in defeat, real grace, can be more inspiring than a victory.

"Do not come any closer," God said. "Take off your sandals,
for the place where you are standing is holy ground."
EXODUS 3:5 NIV

862 When your family—no matter what you might have contributed—is known locally as "good people." It's a label you might rebel against briefly, but it's a tradition well worth carrying on. And it's a gift from your ancestors who never got to meet you.

863 If you listen to the stories of people who have lost wallets or purses in the past, you would think nothing was ever returned. But when yours gets returned, almost everyone has a similar story of honesty to share. We seem to expect the worst despite the fact that the best keeps breaking through.

864 An Olympic swimmer who was coached by her father shared the last words he told her before each race. "He tells me he loves me." Love! Despite the world's efforts to tell you different, it's still the greatest motivator ever.

Try to imagine how your family, in generations gone by, was seen by their neighbors. Write about any individuals you know of who may have contributed to that:

....

....

....

....

....

....

....

....

....

....

....

....

....

....

....

....

....

And the ark of God remained with the family of Obededom in his house three months. And the Lord blessed the house of Obededom, and all that he had.

1 Chronicles 13:14 KJV

Write about innocence, what it means to you. And give some examples:

....

....

....

....

....

....

....

....

....

....

....

....

....

....

....

....

....

....

....

....

....

865 The woman who walked the city streets with a sandwich board. Eschewing the usual message of doom and gloom, her simple sign said Trust In Kindness. When people smiled, she smiled back and said, "That's why I'm doing this."

866 The beggar who looked like his situation might be self-inflicted. The man who gave him money and, in a choked voice, said, "Because you could be my son." The woman who, seeing this, gave more than she had planned and told him, "Do something to make your mother and father proud."

867 The way everyone is included and everyone is welcome to join in when little girls hold hands and dance in a circle.

When Pilate saw that he could prevail nothing, but that rather a tumult was made, he took water, and washed his hands before the multitude, saying, I am innocent of the blood of this just person: see ye to it.

MATTHEW 27:24 KJV

868 Watching youngsters face the fear of doing something good they haven't done before and doing it anyway. There are great things waiting for those who can step through that phony barrier.

869 "Aunt Annie" who was the best singer in her family. She only had an okay voice and she never remembered all the lyrics, but it was always her who started the song for others to join in with. The world needs people to start the songs.

870 That there are more encouragers out there than any of us will ever know. Like Tom and Sue sitting in their garden listening to a distant trumpeter repeatedly trying to master a difficult tune. Each time he reaches the tricky bit they quietly insist, "You can do it this time!"

Write about an unusual or inspiring way someone found to be encouraging:

....
....
....
....
....
....
....
....
....
....
....
....
....
....
....
....
....
....

Then tidings of these things came unto the ears of the church which was in Jerusalem: and they sent forth Barnabas, that he should go as far as Antioch. Who, when he came, and had seen the grace of God, was glad, and exhorted them all, that with purpose of heart they would cleave unto the Lord.

ACTS 11:22–23 KJV

Write about a time you saw your home or hometown or country through the eyes of a visitor. What surprised you?

....

....

....

....

....

....

....

....

....

....

871 It's just a suggestion with no scientific proof, but the more you teach children to encourage others, the less help you will find they need with the ordinary things in life. It's as if they already have their own internal cheer squad!

872 We may have successfully packed our own conscience away where it can't be heard, but a child who hasn't yet learned cynicism makes a fine substitute.

873 Visitors to your hometown are the most effective way of seeing it through fresh eyes.

....

....

....

....

....

....

....

....

....

Now therefore ye are no more strangers and foreigners,
but fellow citizens with the saints, and of the household of God.
Ephesians 2:19 KJV

874 "The people have to want to come. The weather reports will be a factor. The roads and railways have to be open. And the ferry has to be operating. And if I can sell them some ice cream when they get here…" A sweet example from a tourist destination of how interconnected we all are.

875 Blessed are the peacemakers—like when twin two-year-old girls were fighting in the mall and ignoring their mom. A passerby, a silversmith, gave the mom a necklace she had been working on. The dispute instantly forgotten, the girls joined their mom in oohing over the gift.

876 A definition of family worth considering: "It's not the ones you are related to; it's the ones who hold your hand when you need it most."

Write about a surprising connection you discovered between you and someone else:

....

....

....

....

....

....

....

....

....

....

....

....

....

....

....

....

....

....

....

....

For through him we both have access by one Spirit unto the Father.
EPHESIANS 2:18 KJV

Write about a time you saw a child instinctively following the example of someone older:

....

....

....

....

....

....

....

....

....

....

....

....

....

....

....

....

....

....

....

....

....

877   On the night before a birthday, a mom asked for one last look at her ten-year-old. "The ten-year-old will still be there, Mom," the daughter reassured her. "Just a layer away." What a blessing for those with more than eleven layers to think that all those ages are still there.

878   Reporting on a sincere apology and the response it provoked, a reporter said, "Most of us owe at least one and most are due at least one. Either way, they have the power to turn a life around." Or maybe two.

879   The way little girls will be entranced by bigger girls, and boys will hero worship young men.

Be ye imitators of me, even as I also am of Christ.
1 CORINTHIANS 11:1 ASV

880 The old man who couldn't get to the river anymore but had taught his son to love fishing. Now the son was teaching the grandchildren. Health comes and goes, but families, and the traditions they carry, go on like a river.

881 David Gamut from *The Last of the Mohicans* was not a warrior. Rather than taking to arms, he sang psalms in battle. The Hurons thought him crazy, or talking to God, so they left him alone. There are better ways to fight. Sing praises instead of battle songs.

882 A wise man wrote that the road to heaven isn't long or far away but has rocks on it we need to move. The rocks are real, earthly things like giving or taking offense, not loving justice, or whatever separates people from each other. And each of them can be lifted by the weakest of us.

Write about the song (hymn or otherwise) that brings you closest to God, peace, and love:

....

....

....

....

....

....

....

....

....

....

....

....

....

....

....

....

....

....

....

....

....

....

....

Sing to the LORD a new song; sing to the LORD, all the earth. Sing to the LORD, praise his name; proclaim his salvation day after day.

PSALM 96:1–2 NIV

Write about how you respond to kindnesses:

....

....

....

....

....

....

....

....

....

....

....

....

....

....

....

....

....

....

....

....

....

883 The photographer who saw the bride-to-be's neighbor hurriedly tidying her garden, "So there won't be weeds in her wedding photos." The bride-to-be was blissfully unaware—but how often are we helped like that, in ways we don't know about?

884 Gift giving can be a real art, but it can be expensive. Far less expensive is the art of gift receiving. It costs nothing, but done properly, it can leave the giver feeling they have also received.

885 Every time someone has a chance to take advantage of your lack of knowledge, your distractedness, your carelessness…and doesn't.

I am not worthy of the least of all the lovingkindnesses, and of all the truth, which thou hast showed unto thy servant; for with my staff I passed over this Jordan; and now I am become two companies.

GENESIS 32:10 ASV

886 Coming home after being away for an extended period—and everything being just as you left it. It's a comforting feeling.

887 Coming home after being away for an extended period—and almost nothing being as you left it, because your home is a living and thriving place.

888 Complaining on the phone about the state of the world while withdrawing cash from an ATM. Then having someone chase after you with the cash you left in the machine. "I see what you did there, God!"

Write about coming home—how it is and how you would like it to be:

....

....

....

....

....

....

....

....

....

....

....

....

....

....

....

....

....

....

....

....

....

And Jesus saith unto him, The foxes have holes, and the birds of the heaven have nests; but the Son of man hath not where to lay his head.

MATTHEW 8:20 ASV

Write about your hopes for the future:

....

....

....

....

....

....

....

....

....

....

....

....

....

....

....

....

....

....

....

....

889 A gift from someone who doesn't have much to give.

890 Seeing youngsters actively trying to make their way in the world—especially if they are cooperating or working on something for the common good. Their drive and principles are the future.

891 That if you sneeze almost anywhere in the English-speaking word, someone will probably say, "Bless you!"

"For I know the plans I have for you, declares the LORD, plans for welfare and not for evil, to give you a future and a hope."

JEREMIAH 29:11 ESV

892 Milestone birthdays—a good excuse to thank everyone who helped you get that far in a life that few would get through without a support network.

893 Support networks—especially the ones based on friendship, faith, and family.

894 George Washington asked a man why he had asked him for help. "Because you have a 'yes' face," the man is supposed to have said. A "yes face" might be a burden, but it is also, undoubtedly, a blessing.

Write about your support network (or one you would like to set up):

....

....

....

....

....

....

....

....

....

....

....

....

....

....

....

....

....

....

....

....

In the midst of a very severe trial, their overflowing joy and their extreme poverty welled up in rich generosity. For I testify that they gave as much as they were able, and even beyond their ability. Entirely on their own, they urgently pleaded with us for the privilege of sharing in this service to the Lord's people.

2 CORINTHIANS 8:2–4 NIV

Write about your secret(s) of happiness:

....

....

....

....

....

....

....

....

....

....

....

....

....

....

....

....

....

....

....

....

....

....

895 The secret of happiness—and the many wonderful things you get to try out before you discover it.

896 That being a lady, or a gentleman, isn't easy. If it was, everyone would do it, and then it wouldn't be anything special.

897 That in helping others we almost always end up helping ourselves.

Delight thyself also in the LORD:
and he shall give thee the desires of thine heart.
PSALM 37:4 KJV

898 A "gardening" tip from Saint Basil: "If you plant courtesy you reap friendship. If you plant kindness you gather love."

899 An eggshell is a wonder in its own right, so it might be a shame to see one broken. But the result will, usually, have been a chick— an even greater wonder. Don't cry when good things break. Look for the better things they gave birth to.

900 This quote by actress Gillian Anderson: "There is nothing that creates more of a feeling of empowerment than being of service to someone in need."

Write about something you were sad to see go— until you saw what replaced it:

....

....

....

....

....

....

....

....

....

....

....

....

....

....

....

....

....

....

....

....

....

For, behold, I create new heavens and a new earth; and the former things shall not be remembered, nor come into mind.

Isaiah 65:17 ASV

Write about a time someone stepped into your life, briefly took on your role and responsibilities—and did a good job:

....

....

....

....

....

....

....

....

....

....

....

....

....

....

....

....

....

....

....

....

901 Autograph books with messages of love and support from the past.

902 That as cut flowers start to wither, their colors often become more intense.

903 A friend, or friends, you can trust to take good, wise, and discreet care of your mistakes.

I am sending him—who is my very heart—back to you. I would have liked to keep him with me so that he could take your place in helping me while I am in chains for the gospel.
PHILEMON 1:12–13 NIV

904 That when you're having a bad day, you might as well do all those other painful, depressing, or embarrassing things you keep putting off in case you spoil your day. Getting them all done will automatically make it a good day!

905 That Albert Einstein was famously bad at math. Or: it's a wonderful world where we aren't all good (or bad) at the same thing and there is space for each of our talents.

906 That the statue of Peter Pan in London, England, has places where the bronze has been polished golden by the caressing hands of children (of all ages). A gentle touch can do the same to those of us who don't live in Neverland.

Write about an imaginary meeting with a character from a favorite book:

....
....
....
....
....
....
....
....
....
....
....
....
....
....
....
....
....
....
....
....

*Therefore that disciple whom Jesus loved saith unto Peter,
It is the Lord. Now when Simon Peter heard that it was
the Lord, he girt his fisher's coat unto him, (for he was
naked,) and did cast himself into the sea.*

JOHN 21:7 KJV

Write about an encounter with someone whose name you couldn't recall:

....

....

....

....

....

....

....

....

....

....

....

....

....

....

....

....

....

....

....

....

....

907 That many old tapestries have a tangle of broken thread on the back sides, either broken deliberately or because of weaknesses in the thread. But the unbroken ones hold the broken one together.

908 When people you have forgotten don't forget you. (It can be embarrassing, but it's nice.)

909 In a world where we must work, work and the ability to work is a blessing.

He said, "Who are you?" And she answered, "I am Ruth, your servant. Spread your wings over your servant, for you are a redeemer."

RUTH 3:9 ESV

910   Love at first sight…
and second sight…and third
sight…and at every sight of
that one person for the rest
of your life together.

911   That being told you do
something like an amateur
is a good thing. The word
comes from the Latin word
amator and means someone
who does something for love.

912   When someone
sends you an unsigned card
thanking you for your help
and you need to narrow
it down from a long list of
suspects.

Write about the things you do for love that bring
you the greatest pleasure:

....

....

....

....

....

....

....

....

....

....

....

....

....

....

....

....

....

....

....

....

....

*Many waters cannot quench love; rivers cannot sweep
it away. If one were to give all the wealth of one's
house for love, it would be utterly scorned.*

SONG OF SOLOMON 8:7 NIV

Write about a special time as a child when you got to stay up late:

....

....

....

....

....

....

....

....

....

....

....

....

....

....

....

....

....

....

....

....

913 Giving necessities to people in difficult situations is fine, but if you get the chance to also give an "extra," a little luxury, take it. The difference it might make to someone struggling to get by is likely to be beyond words.

914 Understanding that keeping a nice garden isn't only for you; it's for the enjoyment of the whole world should they choose to pass by and look.

915 That the dawn chorus usually begins when it is still dark.

And at midnight there was a cry made,
Behold, the bridegroom cometh; go ye out to meet him.
MATTHEW 25:6 KJV

916   That big jobs can be done in little pieces. (Whether it's something practical like restoring a house or something emotional like restoring a friendship—or a life.)

917   That beauty is such a lifter of the soul.

918   The enthusiasm of dogs reminds us that if a thing's good, it's always good. A walk is good—another walk five minutes later is just as good. It's the same with meals, head rubs, and everything else. Let's be less blasé and wag our tails some more.

Write about a long-term project of yours that finally came to fruition:

....

....

....

....

....

....

....

....

....

....

....

....

....

....

....

....

....

....

....

....

*In the beginning was the Word, and the
Word was with God, and the Word was God.*

JOHN 1:1 ASV

Write about a time you had no idea of the good you were doing—until afterward:

....
....
....
....
....
....
....
....
....
....
....
....
....

919 Discovering why rude and unpleasant people are rude and unpleasant. It will often be heartbreaking—but it will help you love them.

920 Small, door-shaped gaps along the bottom of deer fences (to let the rabbits and squirrels through!).

921 That we never know when someone really, really needs someone to be nice to them. If we did, we might only be nice on those occasions and miss out on the folks who only really needed it, or maybe just needed it. Best to cover all the bases!

....
....
....
....
....
....
....
....
....

Praise be to the God and Father of our Lord Jesus Christ, who has blessed us in the heavenly realms with every spiritual blessing in Christ.

EPHESIANS 1:3 NIV

922 That butterfly wings are often dull on the underside. A reminder of how beautiful we appear to someone looking down from above.

923 That strong winds make for deep roots, and tough times grow resilient people.

924 That when you put your best into doing something, you will often be surprised by how good that is.

Compile a random list of happy childhood memories (and share them with a parent, sibling, or someone else who was around then):

....

....

....

....

....

....

....

....

....

....

....

....

....

....

....

....

....

....

....

He redeemed us in order that the blessing given to Abraham might come to the Gentiles through Christ Jesus, so that by faith we might receive the promise of the Spirit.

GALATIANS 3:14 NIV

Write about the person (relative, neighbor, teacher...) you aspired to be like when you were a child:

....

....

....

....

....

....

....

....

....

....

....

....

....

....

....

....

....

....

....

925 The way young married couples give a romantic boost to people who have been married for decades. And older married couples give the youngsters proof that happily-ever-afters do exist.

926 That kindness inspires other people to be kind, which inspires other people to be kind, which inspires...

927 When a stranger looks into your life for a moment and comments on how much you are loved. We take things for granted, and it's nice to be reminded of the important stuff from time to time.

The people were amazed at his teaching, because he taught them as one who had authority, not as the teachers of the law.

MARK 1:22 NIV

928 Messages—texts, emails, postcards, letters, etc.—that don't actually have any point to them. But they mean someone is thinking of you.

929 Just because you can do a thing doesn't mean you need to.

930 When tripping and falling at the beginning of a run gives you the determination to do a better time than you might otherwise. (This doesn't just apply to running—but you knew that already!)

Write about an unusual spur that made you more determined to do something:

....

....

....

....

....

....

....

....

....

....

....

....

....

....

....

....

....

....

....

I long to see you so that I may impart to you some spiritual gift to make you strong—that is, that you and I may be mutually encouraged by each other's faith.

ROMANS 1:11–12 NIV

Write about the most memorable (for a good reason) party you ever attended:

....
....
....
....
....
....
....
....
....
....
....
....
....
....
....
....
....
....
....
....
....
....

931 A woman in her sixties who asked her friend for a princess-themed birthday party—then had them take it to the next street for a nine-year-old girl whose parents couldn't afford to throw her any kind of party.

932 For everything or every person that breaks your heart, there will be something or someone out there to make it sing again.

933 Mothers who put up with their little sons' clumsy attempts at being helpful gentlemen—for the sake of someone she hasn't yet met, the woman he might someday marry.

And all the people went their way to eat, and to drink,
and to send portions, and to make great mirth, because they
had understood the words that were declared unto them.

NEHEMIAH 8:12 KJV

934 "Are you having a good day?" she asked the flower seller. "Life is all good," was the reply. "Don't you have any troubles?" she asked. "Oh, everybody has troubles," the flower seller replied, "but maybe I just wear them well." Wear your troubles well.

935 When a "heart attack" involves decorating someone's room or bathroom mirror with hearts while they are out.

936 In being careful not to do anything wrong we can sometimes forget to live life. There is freedom in these words by the French novelist Collette: "You will do foolish things, but do them with enthusiasm."

Write about a time you did something with foolish enthusiasm:

....
....
....
....
....
....
....
....
....
....
....
....
....
....
....
....
....
....
....

"Lord, if it's you," Peter replied, "tell me to come to you on the water." "Come," he said. Then Peter got down out of the boat, walked on the water and came toward Jesus.

MATTHEW 14:28–29 NIV

Write about how you thought love would be before you found it—and how it actually is:

....
....
....
....
....
....
....
....
....
....
....
....
....
....
....
....
....
....
....
....
....

937 The fact that airplanes will usually tend to right themselves after turbulence. They are actually designed to "straighten up and fly right." And so are we.

938 Negative people— because they make positive people try so much harder!

939 The handwritten message inside the valentine card read "Love you more than sixty-four." It turned out, 1964 was the year they married. The blessing? That love grows!

Love suffereth long, and is kind; love envieth not; love vaunteth not itself, is not puffed up, doth not behave itself unseemly, seeketh not its own, is not provoked, taketh not account of evil.

1 CORINTHIANS 13:4–5 ASV

940 The blind man pushing the wheelchair while the woman in it gives him directions and a running commentary on everything and everyone she sees. We are better together.

941 Revisiting the place where he first told you he loved you—or where he asked that question.

942 Being a child and watching your mother do… anything. There's a certainty and a smoothness about how she works that you could never imagine you would achieve—until you see your child watching you, and you realize…

Write about an example of interdependence that touched your heart:

....
....
....
....
....
....
....
....
....
....
....
....
....
....
....
....
....
....

With great power the apostles continued to testify to the resurrection of the Lord Jesus. And God's grace was so powerfully at work in them all that there were no needy persons among them. For from time to time those who owned land or houses sold them, brought the money from the sales and put it at the apostles' feet, and it was distributed to anyone who had need.

ACTS 4:33–35 NIV

Describe your personal idea of peace:

....
....
....
....
....
....
....
....
....
....
....
....
....
....
....
....
....
....
....

943 Watching a child sleep, clutching their "blankie." As well as being a moment of peace, it's a reminder that we were made to hold on to something, or Someone.

944 If it comes down to the choice between being right or being kind, be kind—and you will be right.

945 People guaranteed to answer your call. Or, if they can't answer it right away they will call you back ASAP. (Which also says something good about the kind of person you are!)

In peace will I both lay me down and sleep;
for thou, Jehovah, alone makest me dwell in safety.

PSALM 4:8 ASV

946 The wind whispering through a cornfield. There are places you may never go (like into the middle of the corn—unless you're a farmer), but the breeze goes to all those places. Like God in our lives.

947 A shared umbrella.

948 There's an island off the coast of Scotland that is officially surrounded by the Atlantic Ocean—but the mainland is only yards away. You can cross the Atlantic there by bridge. You can do great things and overcome huge obstacles by finding the right bridge.

Write about a novel or imaginative way you, or a friend, overcame a problem:

....
....
....
....
....
....
....
....
....
....
....
....
....
....
....
....
....
....
....
....
....

And he said, Thy name shall be called no more Jacob, but Israel:
for thou hast striven with God and with men, and hast prevailed.

GENESIS 32:28 ASV

Write about a promise to the future you made and kept:

....

....

....

....

....

....

....

....

....

....

....

....

....

....

....

....

....

....

....

....

949 Waterfalls. They can take a real tumble, be spun around by the shock when they hit the bottom— but then they bring it all together and carry on. Smoothly and serenely.

950 What would your today say to your tomorrow? To a large degree it's up to us whether the answer would be "I'm sorry" or "You're welcome!"

951 If you're at a point where you can't pray, you can recite the alphabet and trust God to rearrange the letters into the right words.

He is the Lord our God; his judgments are in all the earth. He remembers his covenant forever, the promise he made, for a thousand generations.

PSALM 105:7–8 NIV

952 That so many of the practical, everyday things people do for us have love behind them, so don't just say thank you for the thing that was done; appreciate why it was done as well.

953 The word *mercy* in the Bible is usually translated from the Hebrew word *chesed*, which means "God's enduring love."

954 You know the phrase "It doesn't get any better than this!" That's a good way of showing appreciation, but the truth is…it does! And it will!

Write about the different kinds of love that make themselves felt in your life:

....

....

....

....

....

....

....

....

....

....

....

....

....

....

....

....

....

....

....

....

And now these three remain: faith, hope and love.
But the greatest of these is love.
1 Corinthians 13:13 NIV

Write about a personal mantra, prayer, or technique you use for rising above the clouds of life:

....

....

....

....

....

....

....

....

....

....

....

....

....

....

....

....

....

....

955 You ask God for a sign and nothing changes— because it's all a sign! (Like the joke where the fish says, "Wet? What does 'wet' mean?" He's so surrounded by wet he isn't aware of it. Same with us and signs.)

956 The fact that the sun shines every day, whether it's cloudy or not. What we have to do is find ways to rise above our personal clouds to the sunshine that is waiting for us.

957 Driftwood used as art-work. How did the wood get that smooth, flowing, elegant look? Tides and storms. Just like you did.

Grace to you and peace be multiplied in the knowledge of God and of Jesus our Lord; seeing that his divine power hath granted unto us all things that pertain unto life and godliness, through the knowledge of him that called us by his own glory and virtue.

2 Peter 1:2–3 ASV

958 "Pooh-sticks." Dropping sticks, leaves, or flowers off one side of a bridge and rushing to the other side to see whose "boat" comes out first. A fun example of finding beauty and peace in little, inconsequential things.

959 Doing something, usually something difficult, that every fiber of your being knows is right and good.

960 The people who respond in a huge variety of ways to a huge variety of disasters and the like. The "helpers" as Mr. Rogers's mom called them.

Write about a disaster that provoked a positive response in you:

....
....
....
....
....
....
....
....
....
....
....
....
....
....
....
....
....
....
....
....
....
....

That is why, for Christ's sake, I delight in weaknesses,
in insults, in hardships, in persecutions, in difficulties.
For when I am weak, then I am strong.
2 CORINTHIANS 12:10 NIV

Write about a token of love you gave or received:

....

....

....

....

....

....

....

....

....

....

....

....

....

....

....

....

....

....

....

....

....

961 When someone makes a space for you at a crowded gathering. The feeling of inclusion is a beautiful thing to receive—and to give!

962 That no matter how bad the day was, the next day will be greeted by birds singing! Feel free to join them.

963 Tokens of love and how they can be anything at all—so long as they mean something to you and your love.

For God so loved the world that he gave his one and only Son,
that whoever believes in him shall not perish but have eternal life.

JOHN 3:16 NIV

964 That—more than you may think—you don't go to wonderful places; you take the wonderful with you!

965 The woman in the busy coffee shop who overheard the angry words, "If you don't like it, you know what you can do!" Distracted, she took a sip of coffee and it was bitter. So, she added the forgotten sweetener and thought, *Yeah. If you don't like it—you can make it better!*

966 She was leaning against his chest when the wheel of the subway car squealed along a stretch of rail. He winced, instinctively raised his hands—and put them over her ears! Being put first. A blessing.

Write about a time your sweetheart put you first:

....
....
....
....
....
....
....
....
....
....
....
....
....
....
....
....
....
....
....
....
....
....
....

"The greatest among you will be your servant.
For those who exalt themselves will be humbled,
and those who humble themselves will be exalted."
MATTHEW 23:11–12 NIV

Write a letter of thanks to your grandparents for something special they did (or to grandchildren for the same thing):

....
....
....
....
....
....
....
....
....
....
....
....
....
....
....
....
....
....
....

967 Grandparents. They have all the love your parents have for you—and more time to show it.

968 *Floccinaucinihilipilification* is one of the longest words in the English language. It means "the habit of estimating something as worthless." Never heard of it? Perhaps that's because nothing is worthless— except perhaps the word *floccinaucinihilipilification*.

969 They say the hole in the middle of a good dream catcher is to let the bad dreams pass through. You are blessed indeed if you also have a way of letting bad pass through and fall behind while catching and keeping the good.

"From now on all generations will call me blessed, for the Mighty One has done great things for me—holy is his name."
LUKE 1:48–49 NIV

970 That there is a God. Otherwise we would have no one to thank for this wonderful world.

971 The chapel in Yosemite National Park has plain glass windows instead of ornate stained glass because there is more beauty outside than could ever be depicted in a window. It's not just like that in Yosemite. Look around!

972 Being helped by someone who is only in the position to do so because you once helped them.

Write about a positive example of "what goes around comes around":

....

....

....

....

....

....

....

....

....

....

....

....

....

....

....

....

....

....

....

....

....

*After Job had prayed for his friends, the LORD restored his
fortunes and gave him twice as much as he had before.*

JOB 42:10 NIV

Write about the first gift you can remember being given:

....
....
....
....
....
....
....
....
....
....
....
....
....
....
....
....
....
....
....
....

973   Gifts of love. Like when eight-year-old Morag asked for a baby doll after seeing one in a catalog. Her mother painted a face on a brick and wrapped it in a blanket. It was all she could afford. Eighty years later Morag sighed happily, remembering her first baby.

974   To paraphrase John Gardner from LBJ's administration, "Whoever you are and whatever you are doing, some kind of excellence is within your reach."

975 You love your family with ALL your heart. Then a new little addition comes along and, amazingly, you still have a heart full of love to give them. In the same way God loves each of us with ALL of His heart.

Then Peter said unto them, Repent, and be baptized every one of you in the name of Jesus Christ for the remission of sins, and ye shall receive the gift of the Holy Ghost.

ACTS 2:38 KJV

976 Still holding hands after decades of marriage.

977 The Irish have a proverb—"It is in the shelter of each other that we live." If you have a good shelter, you are blessed. If you can also be a shelter, then you are doubly so.

978 The years you had nothing. Except love.

Write about the single thing you think contributes most to a happy relationship:

....
....
....
....
....
....
....
....
....
....
....
....
....
....
....
....
....
....
....

Let the husband render unto the wife due benevolence:
and likewise also the wife unto the husband.

1 CORINTHIANS 7:3 KJV

Write about the things you make with your hands:

....
....
....
....
....
....
....
....
....
....
....
....
....
....
....
....
....
....
....
....
....
....

979 That 40 percent of your worries are just because you're tired, 30 percent you can't help, 12 percent are other people's business, 10 percent are to do with health, which only gets worse when you worry, and 8 percent are real, but you can only tackle them after dumping the rest. So dump the rest.

980 National Geographic ran a story about a cat that walked side by side with a blind friend, guiding it through their intertwining tails. We have the blessing of hands. How much more might we do with them?

981 Standing on a hilltop (physical or metaphorical), for the view and for the fact that you made the climb all the way.

And the eyes of them both were opened, and they knew that they were naked; and they sewed fig-leaves together, and made themselves aprons.

GENESIS 3:7 ASV

982　When someone thanks you again for a long-ago favor and you don't remember it, but it sounds like the kind of thing you would have done.

983　The couple you think shouldn't work—but they do! It shows there is hope, and love, for all of us.

984　That we do not have as much as we might wish for, so we are not distracted from the value of what we do have.

Write about an "odd couple" and how such different people are often so right for each other:

....

....

....

....

....

....

....

....

....

....

....

....

....

....

....

....

....

....

....

And she had a sister called Mary, which also sat at Jesus' feet, and heard his word. But Martha was cumbered about much serving, and came to him, and said, Lord, dost thou not care that my sister hath left me to serve alone? bid her therefore that she help me.

LUKE 10:39–40 KJV

Write about a piece of art that speaks to you in some way:

....
....
....
....
....
....
....
....
....
....
....
....
....
....
....
....
....
....
....
....
....

985 That we usually do not have a fair share of the troubles in the world.

986 Supportive traveling companions. Like Jack and Ian, who normally hold walking sticks in their left hands. The other day, Jack swapped the stick to his right hand, then he and Ian linked their free arms and off they went.

987 That you can be a great artist without picking up a paintbrush. Vincent Van Gogh, who knew a thing or two about art, said, "There is nothing more artistic than to love others."

I do all this for the sake of the gospel,
that I may share in its blessings.
1 CORINTHIANS 9:23 NIV

988 That understanding comes in stages and at different ages. (Can you imagine what hard work teenagers would be if they really knew everything?)

989 That you and your partner don't always agree with each other. Because if you did, as Ruth Bell Graham said, there would be no need for one of you. (And there is need for both of you, which is a blessing.)

990 Being able to say thank you, having things to say thank you for, the good feeling that comes with saying thank you, the way you make others feel when you say thank you… Thank You, Lord, for all those blessings in two little words.

Write about a moment of understanding that came later in life (than your teens):

....
....
....
....
....
....
....
....
....
....
....
....
....
....
....
....
....
....

Who is wise and understanding among you?
Let them show it by their good life, by deeds
done in the humility that comes from wisdom.

JAMES 3:13 NIV

Write about the different ways you have heard (or seen) people say (or demonstrate) "I love you":

....

....

....

....

....

....

....

....

....

....

....

....

....

....

....

....

....

....

....

....

....

991   People will tell you they like you or love you in a variety of ways, depending on their hearts and abilities. Having the insight to recognize the real feeling behind an unorthodox presentation is a real blessing in a damaged world.

992   Humility is a blessing (although trying to be the most humble kind of misses the point!).

993   The firefighter (and people like him) who was fined for losing his ax while saving a life and promised he would do the same the next time.

Jesus straightened up and asked her, "Woman, where are they? Has no one condemned you?" "No one, sir," she said. "Then neither do I condemn you," Jesus declared. "Go now and leave your life of sin."

JOHN 8:10–11 NIV

994 The feeling you have when you are so full of love and happiness that you are convinced your work here is done and God can take you home anytime.

995 Laying down whatever "weapons" you have and living in trust.

996 The Bible Hilda's father gave her in 1927 and inside which he wrote the advice he hoped would see her safely through this world to the next—"Love one another."

Write about a time you were vulnerable. Where did the strength come from when it came?

....
....
....
....
....
....
....
....
....
....
....
....
....
....
....
....
....
....

But he said to me, "My grace is sufficient for you, for my power is made perfect in weakness." Therefore I will boast all the more gladly about my weaknesses, so that Christ's power may rest on me.

2 CORINTHIANS 12:9 NIV

Write about a beautiful beginning:

....
....
....
....
....
....
....
....
....
....
....
....
....
....
....
....
....
....
....
....
....

997 We are blessed with truths that stand the test of time.

998 "Eyes to see" are a blessing. They enable us to see that the world is full of blessings!

999 The moment when something comes to an end. Bless it, value it, take its lessons on board. Then turn toward the new beginning and all of its wonderful possibilities.

Therefore if any man be in Christ, he is a new creature: old things are passed away; behold, all things are become new.

2 CORINTHIANS 5:17 KJV

1,000 God came down to earth as a little baby.

Write a thank-you to the Lord:

....
....
....
....
....
....
....
....
....
....
....
....
....
....
....
....
....
....
....
....
....

And she shall bring forth a son, and thou shalt call his name JESUS:
for he shall save his people from their sins.

MATTHEW 1:21 KJV

Read through the Bible in a Year

1-Jan	Gen. 1-2	Matt. 1	Ps. 1
2-Jan	Gen. 3-4	Matt. 2	Ps. 2
3-Jan	Gen. 5-7	Matt. 3	Ps. 3
4-Jan	Gen. 8-10	Matt. 4	Ps. 4
5-Jan	Gen. 11-13	Matt. 5:1-20	Ps. 5
6-Jan	Gen. 14-16	Matt. 5:21-48	Ps. 6
7-Jan	Gen. 17-18	Matt. 6:1-18	Ps. 7
8-Jan	Gen. 19-20	Matt. 6:19-34	Ps. 8
9-Jan	Gen. 21-23	Matt. 7:1-11	Ps. 9:1-8
10-Jan	Gen. 24	Matt. 7:12-29	Ps. 9:9-20
11-Jan	Gen. 25-26	Matt. 8:1-17	Ps. 10:1-11
12-Jan	Gen. 27:1-28:9	Matt. 8:18-34	Ps. 10:12-18
13-Jan	Gen. 28:10-29:35	Matt. 9	Ps. 11
14-Jan	Gen. 30:1-31:21	Matt. 10:1-15	Ps. 12
15-Jan	Gen. 31:22-32:21	Matt. 10:16-36	Ps. 13
16-Jan	Gen. 32:22-34:31	Matt. 10:37-11:6	Ps. 14
17-Jan	Gen. 35-36	Matt. 11:7-24	Ps. 15
18-Jan	Gen. 37-38	Matt. 11:25-30	Ps. 16
19-Jan	Gen. 39-40	Matt. 12:1-29	Ps. 17
20-Jan	Gen. 41	Matt. 12:30-50	Ps. 18:1-15
21-Jan	Gen. 42-43	Matt. 13:1-9	Ps. 18:16-29
22-Jan	Gen. 44-45	Matt. 13:10-23	Ps. 18:30-50
23-Jan	Gen. 46:1-47:26	Matt. 13:24-43	Ps. 19
24-Jan	Gen. 47:27-49:28	Matt. 13:44-58	Ps. 20
25-Jan	Gen. 49:29-Exod. 1:22	Matt. 14	Ps. 21
26-Jan	Exod. 2-3	Matt. 15:1-28	Ps. 22:1-21
27-Jan	Exod. 4:1-5:21	Matt. 15:29-16:12	Ps. 22:22-31
28-Jan	Exod. 5:22-7:24	Matt. 16:13-28	Ps. 23
29-Jan	Exod. 7:25-9:35	Matt. 17:1-9	Ps. 24
30-Jan	Exod. 10-11	Matt. 17:10-27	Ps. 25
31-Jan	Exod. 12	Matt. 18:1-20	Ps. 26
1-Feb	Exod. 13-14	Matt. 18:21-35	Ps. 27
2-Feb	Exod. 15-16	Matt. 19:1-15	Ps. 28
3-Feb	Exod. 17-19	Matt. 19:16-30	Ps. 29
4-Feb	Exod. 20-21	Matt. 20:1-19	Ps. 30
5-Feb	Exod. 22-23	Matt. 20:20-34	Ps. 31:1-8
6-Feb	Exod. 24-25	Matt. 21:1-27	Ps. 31:9-18
7-Feb	Exod 26-27	Matt. 21:28-46	Ps. 31:19-24
8-Feb	Exod. 28	Matt. 22	Ps. 32
9-Feb	Exod. 29	Matt. 23:1-36	Ps. 33:1-12
10-Feb	Exod. 30-31	Matt. 23:37-24:28	Ps. 33:13-22
11-Feb	Exod. 32-33	Matt. 24:29-51	Ps. 34:1-7
12-Feb	Exod. 34:1-35:29	Matt. 25:1-13	Ps. 34:8-22
13-Feb	Exod. 35:30-37:29	Matt. 25:14-30	Ps. 35:1-8
14-Feb	Exod. 38-39	Matt. 25:31-46	Ps. 35:9-17
15-Feb	Exod. 40	Matt. 26:1-35	Ps. 35:18-28
16-Feb	Lev. 1-3	Matt. 26:36-68	Ps. 36:1-6

17-Feb	Lev. 4:1-5:13	Matt. 26:69-27:26	Ps. 36:7-12
18-Feb	Lev. 5:14 -7:21	Matt. 27:27-50	Ps. 37:1-6
19-Feb	Lev. 7:22-8:36	Matt. 27:51-66	Ps. 37:7-26
20-Feb	Lev. 9-10	Matt. 28	Ps. 37:27-40
21-Feb	Lev. 11-12	Mark 1:1-28	Ps. 38
22-Feb	Lev. 13	Mark 1:29-39	Ps. 39
23-Feb	Lev. 14	Mark 1:40-2:12	Ps. 40:1-8
24-Feb	Lev. 15	Mark 2:13-3:35	Ps. 40:9-17
25-Feb	Lev. 16-17	Mark 4:1-20	Ps. 41:1-4
26-Feb	Lev. 18-19	Mark 4:21-41	Ps. 41:5-13
27-Feb	Lev. 20	Mark 5	Ps. 42-43
28-Feb	Lev. 21-22	Mark 6:1-13	Ps. 44
1-Mar	Lev. 23-24	Mark 6:14-29	Ps. 45:1-5
2-Mar	Lev. 25	Mark 6:30-56	Ps. 45:6-12
3-Mar	Lev. 26	Mark 7	Ps. 45:13-17
4-Mar	Lev. 27	Mark 8	Ps. 46
5-Mar	Num. 1-2	Mark 9:1-13	Ps. 47
6-Mar	Num. 3	Mark 9:14-50	Ps. 48:1-8
7-Mar	Num. 4	Mark 10:1-34	Ps. 48:9-14
8-Mar	Num. 5:1-6:21	Mark 10:35-52	Ps. 49:1-9
9-Mar	Num. 6:22-7:47	Mark 11	Ps. 49:10-20
10-Mar	Num. 7:48-8:4	Mark 12:1-27	Ps. 50:1-15
11-Mar	Num. 8:5-9:23	Mark 12:28-44	Ps. 50:16-23
12-Mar	Num. 10-11	Mark 13:1-8	Ps. 51:1-9
13-Mar	Num. 12-13	Mark 13:9-37	Ps. 51:10-19
14-Mar	Num. 14	Mark 14:1-31	Ps. 52
15-Mar	Num. 15	Mark 14:32-72	Ps. 53
16-Mar	Num. 16	Mark 15:1-32	Ps. 54
17-Mar	Num. 17-18	Mark 15:33-47	Ps. 55
18-Mar	Num. 19-20	Mark 16	Ps. 56:1-7
19-Mar	Num. 21:1-22:20	Luke 1:1-25	Ps. 56:8-13
20-Mar	Num. 22:21-23:30	Luke 1:26-56	Ps. 57
21-Mar	Num. 24-25	Luke 1:57-2:20	Ps. 58
22-Mar	Num. 26:1-27:11	Luke 2:21-38	Ps. 59:1-8
23-Mar	Num. 27:12-29:11	Luke 2:39-52	Ps. 59:9-17
24-Mar	Num. 29:12-30:16	Luke 3	Ps. 60:1-5
25-Mar	Num. 31	Luke 4	Ps. 60:6-12
26-Mar	Num. 32-33	Luke 5:1-16	Ps. 61
27-Mar	Num. 34-36	Luke 5:17-32	Ps. 62:1-6
28-Mar	Deut. 1:1-2:25	Luke 5:33-6:11	Ps. 62:7-12
29-Mar	Deut. 2:26-4:14	Luke 6:12-35	Ps. 63:1-5
30-Mar	Deut. 4:15-5:22	Luke 6:36-49	Ps. 63:6-11
31-Mar	Deut. 5:23-7:26	Luke 7:1-17	Ps. 64:1-5
1-Apr	Deut. 8-9	Luke 7:18-35	Ps. 64:6-10
2-Apr	Deut. 10-11	Luke 7:36-8:3	Ps. 65:1-8
3-Apr	Deut. 12-13	Luke 8:4-21	Ps. 65:9-13
4-Apr	Deut. 14:1-16:8	Luke 8:22-39	Ps. 66:1-7

5-Apr	Deut. 16:9-18:22	Luke 8:40-56	Ps. 66:8-15
6-Apr	Deut. 19:1-21:9	Luke 9:1-22	Ps. 66:16-20
7-Apr	Deut. 21:10-23:8	Luke 9:23-42	Ps. 67
8-Apr	Deut. 23:9-25:19	Luke 9:43-62	Ps. 68:1-6
9-Apr	Deut. 26:1-28:14	Luke 10:1-20	Ps. 68:7-14
10-Apr	Deut. 28:15-68	Luke 10:21-37	Ps. 68:15-19
11-Apr	Deut. 29-30	Luke 10:38-11:23	Ps. 68:20-27
12-Apr	Deut. 31:1-32:22	Luke 11:24-36	Ps. 68:28-35
13-Apr	Deut. 32:23-33:29	Luke 11:37-54	Ps. 69:1-9
14-Apr	Deut. 34-Josh. 2	Luke 12:1-15	Ps. 69:10-17
15-Apr	Josh. 3:1-5:12	Luke 12:16-40	Ps. 69:18-28
16-Apr	Josh. 5:13-7:26	Luke 12:41-48	Ps. 69:29-36
17-Apr	Josh. 8-9	Luke 12:49-59	Ps. 70
18-Apr	Josh. 10:1-11:15	Luke 13:1-21	Ps. 71:1-6
19-Apr	Josh. 11:16-13:33	Luke 13:22-35	Ps. 71:7-16
20-Apr	Josh. 14-16	Luke 14:1-15	Ps. 71:17-21
21-Apr	Josh. 17:1-19:16	Luke 14:16-35	Ps. 71:22-24
22-Apr	Josh. 19:17-21:42	Luke 15:1-10	Ps. 72:1-11
23-Apr	Josh. 21:43-22:34	Luke 15:11-32	Ps. 72:12-20
24-Apr	Josh. 23-24	Luke 16:1-18	Ps. 73:1-9
25-Apr	Judg. 1-2	Luke 16:19-17:10	Ps. 73:10-20
26-Apr	Judg. 3-4	Luke 17:11-37	Ps. 73:21-28
27-Apr	Judg. 5:1-6:24	Luke 18:1-17	Ps. 74:1-3
28-Apr	Judg. 6:25-7:25	Luke 18:18-43	Ps. 74:4-11
29-Apr	Judg. 8:1-9:23	Luke 19:1-28	Ps. 74:12-17
30-Apr	Judg. 9:24-10:18	Luke 19:29-48	Ps. 74:18-23
1-May	Judg. 11:1-12:7	Luke 20:1-26	Ps. 75:1-7
2-May	Judg. 12:8-14:20	Luke 20:27-47	Ps. 75:8-10
3-May	Judg. 15-16	Luke 21:1-19	Ps. 76:1-7
4-May	Judg. 17-18	Luke 21:20-22:6	Ps. 76:8-12
5-May	Judg. 19:1-20:23	Luke 22:7-30	Ps. 77:1-11
6-May	Judg. 20:24-21:25	Luke 22:31-54	Ps. 77:12-20
7-May	Ruth 1-2	Luke 22:55-23:25	Ps. 78:1-4
8-May	Ruth 3-4	Luke 23:26-24:12	Ps. 78:5-8
9-May	1 Sam. 1:1-2:21	Luke 24:13-53	Ps. 78:9-16
10-May	1 Sam. 2:22-4:22	John 1:1-28	Ps. 78:17-24
11-May	1 Sam. 5-7	John 1:29-51	Ps. 78:25-33
12-May	1 Sam. 8:1-9:26	John 2	Ps. 78:34-41
13-May	1 Sam. 9:27-11:15	John 3:1-22	Ps. 78:42-55
14-May	1 Sam. 12-13	John 3:23-4:10	Ps. 78:56-66
15-May	1 Sam. 14	John 4:11-38	Ps. 78:67-72
16-May	1 Sam. 15-16	John 4:39-54	Ps. 79:1-7
17-May	1 Sam. 17	John 5:1-24	Ps. 79:8-13
18-May	1 Sam. 18-19	John 5:25-47	Ps. 80:1-7
19-May	1 Sam. 20-21	John 6:1-21	Ps. 80:8-19
20-May	1 Sam. 22-23	John 6:22-42	Ps. 81:1-10
21-May	1 Sam. 24:1-25:31	John 6:43-71	Ps. 81:11-16

22-May	1 Sam. 25:32-27:12	John 7:1-24	Ps. 82
23-May	1 Sam. 28-29	John 7:25-8:11	Ps. 83
24-May	1 Sam. 30-31	John 8:12-47	Ps. 84:1-4
25-May	2 Sam. 1-2	John 8:48-9:12	Ps. 84:5-12
26-May	2 Sam. 3-4	John 9:13-34	Ps. 85:1-7
27-May	2 Sam. 5:1-7:17	John 9:35-10:10	Ps. 85:8-13
28-May	2 Sam. 7:18-10:19	John 10:11-30	Ps. 86:1-10
29-May	2 Sam. 11:1-12:25	John 10:31-11:16	Ps. 86:11-17
30-May	2 Sam. 12:26-13:39	John 11:17-54	Ps. 87
31-May	2 Sam. 14:1-15:12	John 11:55-12:19	Ps. 88:1-9
1-Jun	2 Sam. 15:13-16:23	John 12:20-43	Ps. 88:10-18
2-Jun	2 Sam. 17:1-18:18	John 12:44-13:20	Ps. 89:1-6
3-Jun	2 Sam. 18:19-19:39	John 13:21-38	Ps. 89:7-13
4-Jun	2 Sam. 19:40-21:22	John 14:1-17	Ps. 89:14-18
5-Jun	2 Sam. 22:1-23:7	John 14:18-15:27	Ps. 89:19-29
6-Jun	2 Sam. 23:8-24:25	John 16:1-22	Ps. 89:30-37
7-Jun	1 Kings 1	John 16:23-17:5	Ps. 89:38-52
8-Jun	1 Kings 2	John 17:6-26	Ps. 90:1-12
9-Jun	1 Kings 3-4	John 18:1-27	Ps. 90:13-17
10-Jun	1 Kings 5-6	John 18:28-19:5	Ps. 91:1-10
11-Jun	1 Kings 7	John 19:6-25a	Ps. 91:11-16
12-Jun	1 Kings 8:1-53	John 19:25b-42	Ps. 92:1-9
13-Jun	1 Kings 8:54-10:13	John 20:1-18	Ps. 92:10-15
14-Jun	1 Kings 10:14-11:43	John 20:19-31	Ps. 93
15-Jun	1 Kings 12:1-13:10	John 21	Ps. 94:1-11
16-Jun	1 Kings 13:11-14:31	Acts 1:1-11	Ps. 94:12-23
17-Jun	1 Kings 15:1-16:20	Acts 1:12-26	Ps. 95
18-Jun	1 Kings 16:21-18:19	Acts 2:1-21	Ps. 96:1-8
19-Jun	1 Kings 18:20-19:21	Acts2:22-41	Ps. 96:9-13
20-Jun	1 Kings 20	Acts 2:42-3:26	Ps. 97:1-6
21-Jun	1 Kings 21:1-22:28	Acts 4:1-22	Ps. 97:7-12
22-Jun	1 Kings 22:29- 2 Kings 1:18	Acts 4:23-5:11	Ps. 98
23-Jun	2 Kings 2-3	Acts 5:12-28	Ps. 99
24-Jun	2 Kings 4	Acts 5:29-6:15	Ps. 100
25-Jun	2 Kings 5:1-6:23	Acts 7:1-16	Ps. 101
26-Jun	2 Kings 6:24-8:15	Acts 7:17-36	Ps. 102:1-7
27-Jun	2 Kings 8:16-9:37	Acts 7:37-53	Ps. 102:8-17
28-Jun	2 Kings 10-11	Acts 7:54-8:8	Ps. 102:18-28
29-Jun	2 Kings 12-13	Acts 8:9-40	Ps. 103:1-9
30-Jun	2 Kings 14-15	Acts 9:1-16	Ps. 103:10-14
1-Jul	2 Kings 16-17	Acts 9:17-31	Ps. 103:15-22
2-Jul	2 Kings 18:1-19:7	Acts 9:32-10:16	Ps. 104:1-9
3-Jul	2 Kings 19:8-20:21	Acts 10:17-33	Ps. 104:10-23
4-Jul	2 Kings 21:1-22:20	Acts 10:34-11:18	Ps. 104: 24-30
5-Jul	2 Kings 23	Acts 11:19-12:17	Ps. 104:31-35

6-Jul	2 Kings 24-25	Acts 12:18-13:13	Ps. 105:1-7
7-Jul	1 Chron. 1-2	Acts 13:14-43	Ps. 105:8-15
8-Jul	1 Chron. 3:1-5:10	Acts 13:44-14:10	Ps. 105:16-28
9-Jul	1 Chron. 5:11-6:81	Acts 14:11-28	Ps. 105:29-36
10-Jul	1 Chron. 7:1-9:9	Acts 15:1-18	Ps. 105:37-45
11-Jul	1 Chron. 9:10-11:9	Acts 15:19-41	Ps. 106:1-12
12-Jul	1 Chron. 11:10-12:40	Acts 16:1-15	Ps. 106:13-27
13-Jul	1 Chron. 13-15	Acts 16:16-40	Ps. 106:28-33
14-Jul	1 Chron. 16-17	Acts 17:1-14	Ps. 106:34-43
15-Jul	1 Chron. 18-20	Acts 17:15-34	Ps. 106:44-48
16-Jul	1 Chron. 21-22	Acts 18:1-23	Ps. 107:1-9
17-Jul	1 Chron. 23-25	Acts 18:24-19:10	Ps. 107:10-16
18-Jul	1 Chron. 26-27	Acts 19:11-22	Ps. 107:17-32
19-Jul	1 Chron. 28-29	Acts 19:23-41	Ps. 107:33-38
20-Jul	2 Chron. 1-3	Acts 20:1-16	Ps. 107:39-43
21-Jul	2 Chron. 4:1-6:11	Acts 20:17-38	Ps. 108
22-Jul	2 Chron. 6:12-7:10	Acts 21:1-14	Ps. 109:1-20
23-Jul	2 Chron. 7:11-9:28	Acts 21:15-32	Ps. 109:21-31
24-Jul	2 Chron. 9:29-12:16	Acts 21:33-22:16	Ps. 110:1-3
25-Jul	2 Chron. 13-15	Acts 22:17-23:11	Ps. 110:4-7
26-Jul	2 Chron. 16-17	Acts 23:12-24:21	Ps. 111
27-Jul	2 Chron. 18-19	Acts 24:22-25:12	Ps. 112
28-Jul	2 Chron. 20-21	Acts 25:13-27	Ps. 113
29-Jul	2 Chron. 22-23	Acts 26	Ps. 114
30-Jul	2 Chron. 24:1-25:16	Acts 27:1-20	Ps. 115:1-10
31-Jul	2 Chron. 25:17-27:9	Acts 27:21-28:6	Ps. 115:11-18
1-Aug	2 Chron. 28:1-29:19	Acts 28:7-31	Ps. 116:1-5
2-Aug	2 Chron. 29:20-30:27	Rom. 1:1-17	Ps. 116:6-19
3-Aug	2 Chron. 31-32	Rom. 1:18-32	Ps. 117
4-Aug	2 Chron. 33:1-34:7	Rom. 2	Ps. 118:1-18
5-Aug	2 Chron. 34:8-35:19	Rom. 3:1-26	Ps. 118:19-23
6-Aug	2 Chron. 35:20-36:23	Rom. 3:27-4:25	Ps. 118:24-29
7-Aug	Ezra 1-3	Rom. 5	Ps. 119:1-8
8-Aug	Ezra 4-5	Rom. 6:1-7:6	Ps. 119:9-16
9-Aug	Ezra 6:1-7:26	Rom. 7:7-25	Ps. 119:17-32
10-Aug	Ezra 7:27-9:4	Rom. 8:1-27	Ps. 119:33-40
11-Aug	Ezra 9:5-10:44	Rom. 8:28-39	Ps. 119:41-64
12-Aug	Neh. 1:1-3:16	Rom. 9:1-18	Ps. 119:65-72
13-Aug	Neh. 3:17-5:13	Rom. 9:19-33	Ps. 119:73-80
14-Aug	Neh. 5:14-7:73	Rom. 10:1-13	Ps. 119:81-88
15-Aug	Neh. 8:1-9:5	Rom. 10:14-11:24	Ps. 119:89-104
16-Aug	Neh. 9:6-10:27	Rom. 11:25-12:8	Ps. 119:105-120
17-Aug	Neh. 10:28-12:26	Rom. 12:9-13:7	Ps. 119:121-128
18-Aug	Neh. 12:27-13:31	Rom. 13:8-14:12	Ps. 119:129-136
19-Aug	Esther 1:1-2:18	Rom. 14:13-15:13	Ps. 119:137-152
20-Aug	Esther 2:19-5:14	Rom. 15:14-21	Ps. 119:153-168

21-Aug	Esther. 6-8	Rom. 15:22-33	Ps. 119:169-176
22-Aug	Esther 9-10	Rom. 16	Ps. 120-122
23-Aug	Job 1-3	1 Cor. 1:1-25	Ps. 123
24-Aug	Job 4-6	1 Cor. 1:26-2:16	Ps. 124-125
25-Aug	Job 7-9	1 Cor. 3	Ps. 126-127
26-Aug	Job 10-13	1 Cor. 4:1-13	Ps. 128-129
27-Aug	Job 14-16	1 Cor. 4:14-5:13	Ps. 130
28-Aug	Job 17-20	1 Cor. 6	Ps. 131
29-Aug	Job 21-23	1 Cor. 7:1-16	Ps. 132
30-Aug	Job 24-27	1 Cor. 7:17-40	Ps. 133-134
31-Aug	Job 28-30	1 Cor. 8	Ps. 135
1-Sep	Job 31-33	1 Cor. 9:1-18	Ps. 136:1-9
2-Sep	Job 34-36	1 Cor. 9:19-10:13	Ps. 136:10-26
3-Sep	Job 37-39	1 Cor. 10:14-11:1	Ps. 137
4-Sep	Job 40-42	1 Cor. 11:2-34	Ps. 138
5-Sep	Eccles. 1:1-3:15	1 Cor. 12:1-26	Ps. 139:1-6
6-Sep	Eccles. 3:16-6:12	1 Cor. 12:27-13:13	Ps. 139:7-18
7-Sep	Eccles. 7:1-9:12	1 Cor. 14:1-22	Ps. 139:19-24
8-Sep	Eccles. 9:13-12:14	1 Cor. 14:23-15:11	Ps. 140:1-8
9-Sep	SS 1-4	1 Cor. 15:12-34	Ps. 140:9-13
10-Sep	SS 5-8	1 Cor. 15:35-58	Ps. 141
11-Sep	Isa. 1-2	1 Cor. 16	Ps. 142
12-Sep	Isa. 3-5	2 Cor. 1:1-11	Ps. 143:1-6
13-Sep	Isa. 6-8	2 Cor. 1:12-2:4	Ps. 143:7-12
14-Sep	Isa. 9-10	2 Cor. 2:5-17	Ps. 144
15-Sep	Isa. 11-13	2 Cor. 3	Ps. 145
16-Sep	Isa. 14-16	2 Cor. 4	Ps. 146
17-Sep	Isa. 17-19	2 Cor. 5	Ps. 147:1-11
18-Sep	Isa. 20-23	2 Cor. 6	Ps. 147:12-20
19-Sep	Isa. 24:1-26:19	2 Cor. 7	Ps. 148
20-Sep	Isa. 26:20-28:29	2 Cor. 8	Ps. 149-150
21-Sep	Isa. 29-30	2 Cor. 9	Prov. 1:1-9
22-Sep	Isa. 31-33	2 Cor. 10	Prov. 1:10-22
23-Sep	Isa. 34-36	2 Cor. 11	Prov. 1:23-26
24-Sep	Isa. 37-38	2 Cor. 12:1-10	Prov. 1:27-33
25-Sep	Isa. 39-40	2 Cor. 12:11-13:14	Prov. 2:1-15
26-Sep	Isa. 41-42	Gal. 1	Prov. 2:16-22
27-Sep	Isa. 43:1-44:20	Gal. 2	Prov. 3:1-12
28-Sep	Isa. 44:21-46:13	Gal. 3:1-18	Prov. 3:13-26
29-Sep	Isa. 47:1-49:13	Gal 3:19-29	Prov. 3:27-35
30-Sep	Isa. 49:14-51:23	Gal 4:1-11	Prov. 4:1-19
1-Oct	Isa. 52-54	Gal. 4:12-31	Prov. 4:20-27
2-Oct	Isa. 55-57	Gal. 5	Prov. 5:1-14
3-Oct	Isa. 58-59	Gal. 6	Prov. 5:15-23
4-Oct	Isa. 60-62	Eph. 1	Prov. 6:1-5
5-Oct	Isa. 63:1-65:16	Eph. 2	Prov. 6:6-19